THE RACIAL POLICIES OF AMERICAN INDUSTRY

REPORT NO. 29

THE NEGRO IN THE LONGSHORE INDUSTRY

by

LESTER RUBIN

with the assistance of

WILLIAM S. SWIFT

Published by

INDUSTRIAL RESEARCH UNIT
The Wharton School
University of Pennsylvania

Distributed by

University of Pennsylvania Press
Philadelphia, Pennsylvania 19174

Library of Congress Catalog Card Number 74-77560
MANUFACTURED IN THE UNITED STATES OF AMERICA
ISBN: 0-8122-9081-X

Foreword

In September 1966, the Ford Foundation announced a major grant to the Industrial Research Unit of the Wharton School to fund studies of the Racial Policies of American Industry. The purpose of the research effort, now in its seventh year, is to determine why some industries are more hospitable to the employment of Negroes than are others, and why some companies within the same industry have vastly different racial employment policies, and to propose appropriate policy.

The studies have proceeded on an industry-by-industry basis under the direction of the undersigned and of Professor Richard L. Rowan. Although the funding from the Ford Foundation ended September 30, 1972, it was decided to continue the series on a limited basis using, where appropriate, other sources of financing. This study of the longshore industry, the twenty-ninth in the series of reports dealing with specific industries, was funded in part by the Ford Foundation, and in part by unrestricted moneys donated from various sources of the Industrial Research Unit for its research programs. Reports already published are listed on the back cover.

In addition to individual industry reports, major studies combining and comparing the findings of the various industry reports are being completed. Volume I, *Negro Employment in Basic Industry*; Volume II, *Negro Employment in Finance*; Volume III, *Negro Employment in Public Utilities*; Volume IV, *Negro Employment in Southern Industry*; Volume V, *Negro Employment in Land and Air Transport*; and Volume VI, *Negro Employment in Retail Trade,* have all been published. The longshore study will be combined with the report dealing with the offshore maritime industry and an updated one on shipbuilding in Volume VII, *Negro Employment in the Maritime Industry,* to be published in 1974.

The Negro in the Longshore Industry was written by Lester Rubin with the assistance of William S. Swift. Dr. Rubin, who is now in government service, received his doctorate from the University of Pennsylvania and completed this study while a Research Associate on the Industrial Research Unit staff. Mr. Swift, who compiled some of the data and wrote part of Chapter

Two, received his M.B.A. in May 1973 from the Graduate Division of the Wharton School. He is now in private industry. Special thanks are also due Mr. John M. Heneghan, Director of the Office of Civil Rights, Maritime Administration, U.S. Department of Commerce, Mr. Eugene Heller, and other members of that staff, for many favors, and much assistance in obtaining information. Numerous company and union officials also provided data, submitted to long interviews, and otherwise were most helpful.

Many other persons assisted in the making of this study. Dr. John R. Coleman, President of Haverford College and former member of the Ford Foundation staff, made the original grant possible. Subsequent grants were greatly furthered by the fine cooperation of Mitchell Sviridoff, Vice-President, and Basil J. Whiting, Program Officer, Social Development. Acknowledgement is also made to the many contributors to the Industrial Research Unit who have made possible its research program, including the continuation of the Racial Policies of American Industry series.

Miss Elsa Klemp, our statistician helped to develop the data used to check the tables. Mrs. Linda Ritch typed the manuscript, Mrs. Ann C. Emerson edited the manuscript and prepared the index, and Mrs. Margaret E. Doyle managed the various administrative details with her usual competence.

Dr. Rubin, as the senior author, is fully responsible for the content. As in most previous reports, the data cited as "in the author's possession" have been carefully authenticated and are on file in the Industrial Research Unit library.

HERBERT R. NORTHRUP, *Director*
Industrial Research Unit
The Wharton School
University of Pennsylvania

Philadelphia
March 1974

TABLE OF CONTENTS

LIST OF TABLES

CHAPTER I

Introduction

Although modern equipment and methods such as containerization have brought changes to the docks, the loading and unloading of ships remains a highly labor intensive industry that depends upon the labor of the longshoremen more than any other factor. Of special significance for the Racial Policies of American Industry series, is the fact that Negroes have always been represented among dockworkers and today are increasing their proportion in this work despite a net decline in the number of longshoremen which has occurred in recent years. Important too for this analysis is the great strength of unionism in this industry and the fact that black workers have played prominent roles in such unions for over a century.

Information for this study was collected from field interviews, court and administrative law cases, and from an examination of the generous literature. The Census of Population statistics provided the basic data base, with supplementary data coming from figures compiled by other government agencies and local and state port organizations. The data developed by the Equal Employment Opportunity Commission, which has been so valuable for other monographs in this series, proved to be of only minor use in this study because of the small size of the firms, the casual nature of the work, and the inappropriateness of the EEOC classifications of longshore work.

As in other monographs in the series, Chapter II discusses the key structural aspects of the industry which impact upon black employment: the nature of the work, employer size and numbers, employment and manpower characteristics, union organization, and industry location. The chapter that follows will, unlike previous monographs, be organized on a geographic basis rather than on a time basis. Each port in the United States has its own characteristics and its own employment history. Similarities can be noted on a regional basis, but there are great differences over a larger geographical area. Therefore, after a discussion of the general picture, the employment status of blacks will be analyzed in each of the country's major ports. In the final chapter, we shall again return to a general examination, summarize the determinants of racial policies, and predict the future course of black employment in the industry.

CHAPTER II

The Longshore Industry

The term "longshoremen" is a contraction of "alongshoremen." Spelled for a time " 'longshoremen," the "a" has been dropped for most of this century. However, the function of the men who work along the shore—or on the docks—has remained the same: to load and to unload ships. Despite some mechanization and methods of improvement, the longshoremen occupy today, as they have for many years, a strategic position astride the crossroads of commerce. The strength of their unions and their wages are symptomatic of their power to halt ocean commerce. Yet, the work remains largely heavy and unskilled, a fact which has contributed to the large black representation in most ports.

It may well have been more accurate in this study to refer to the industry as the "stevedoring industry" rather than the longshore; whereas longshoremen do the loading and unloading, they are employed either by stevedoring concerns—middlemen who contract with ship concerns to provide manpower for loading and unloading—or by those ship concerns who perform their own stevedoring function. Most longshoremen do not have permanent jobs, working for one stevedore or one ship operator.

THE NATURE AND STRUCTURE OF THE INDUSTRY

In the following sections the structure of the industry and the nature of the work itself are described, with special emphasis placed upon the growth of the longshore unions, noting their profound impact on the industry and its racial policies.

Firms in the Industry

A stevedore is either a person or a firm contracting with a ship operator to load or unload a ship in port. This contractor, in essence, agrees to become the middleman between the ship operator and the supply of longshoremen who perform the actual cargo handling. A direct parallel therefore can be drawn between a stevedore and a building trades contractor: each is in business to supply needed labor, yet each maintains a very small permanent work force.

Typically, a stevedoring firm hires longshoremen, usually on a daily basis, from the labor pool of union members. As a result, a firm's labor force varies directly with the amount of work the firm contracts to perform. This, in turn, is a function of port activity. At any given time, a firm may be working several ships or none at all. Therefore, longshoremen are hired as needed by the firm and discharged upon completion of the contract.

The longshore industry closely approximates the economist's concept of perfect competition. Contractors tend to be small in size, large in number, with very little to differentiate one from another. The product sold by the contractor, cargo handling services, is relatively homogeneous since the workers are all drawn from a common labor supply. The technical knowledge required by the industry is gained mainly through actual work experience on the docks and, in most cases, the contractor performs his work using publicly-owned pier facilities furnishing only a small amount of machinery, generally forklifts and the like. Because of the technical knowledge readily available and the small capital investment required, new firms are able to enter the industry with relative ease. These characteristics create a highly competitive, low-profit stevedoring industry.

In principle, firms submit competitive bids on individual contracts, with contracts awarded to the lowest bidders. In practice, all bids are very similar since they are based on the cost of labor, a given variable for each firm in a given area. Contract awards, therefore, tend to be based on long-standing working relationships between ship operators and particular stevedores rather than on pure economic grounds. Generally, a contractor will work for one or, at most, a few shipping lines and operate in only one port or one section of a large port. The number of competing firms operating in a particular port is determined almost entirely by port size and the amount of waterborne commerce moving through the port. In discussing the longshore industry on the West Coast, Hartman noted:

> The number of firms offering cargo-handling services varies with port size. Small ports typically have only one or two stevedoring or terminal companies. The larger ports may have from five to fifteen privately

owned firms engaged in loading and unloading ocean cargoes or providing various dock services. . . . A small number of companies do business in more than one port.[1]

It is also interesting to note that although Negroes have a long history of work in the longshore industry, references cannot be found in the literature attesting to the possibility that Negroes owned and operated stevedoring firms.

There are two types of cargo, general and bulk. As a rule, longshoremen handle only general cargo which is either dry cargo packaged in containers or liquid cargo shipped in barrels. Bulk cargo, on the other hand; is usually dry, uniform, unpackaged cargo, such as ores and grain, and liquid cargo, such as oil and petroleum products. Bulk cargoes require special equipment for loading and unloading and are generally handled outside the port area by industrial employees.

Some of the larger stevedoring firms operate publicly-owned marine terminals under a lease agreement with local or state governments and provide cargo-handling services for the ships using these facilities. In addition to loading and unloading the vessels, these terminal operators sort and store various cargoes and move them between ship and ground transportation. These added functions require a somewhat larger investment in equipment, however, the major capital outlay for land, buildings, and specialized cargo-handling equipment is made by government.

Some of the more important stevedoring firms are those operated by the shipping companies themselves. These companies provide cargo-handling services for their own vessels with some offering their services to other lines. Matson Terminals, a subsidiary of Matson Navigation Company, and Sea-Land are two examples of major shipping companies performing their own stevedoring function. In general, most larger shipping companies maintain their own dock facilities and terminals in at least one port. The smaller companies, however, do not generate sufficient cargo volume in any one port to justify the acquisition of private dock facilities.

Although technological change and its impact upon the longshore industry will be discussed in a following section, it is important to note that the shipping companies who do their own cargo handling have had the greatest impact on the longshore industry because they have been leaders in the introduction of

---

1. Paul T. Hartman, *Collective Bargaining and Productivity* (Berkeley: University of California Press, 1969), p. 12.

new and more efficient cargo-handling methods. It is, therefore, apparent that smaller companies would not be in a position to make the large capital outlays required for the development of, or acquisition of, specialized cargo-handling equipment.

Work Volume

As noted above, the amount of work in the highly labor intensive longshore industry depends entirely on the amount of cargo passing across the docks. This amount of cargo is a function of the level of waterborne commerce which, in turn, is related to the level of activity in the economy. Of course, the level of Negro employment in any port is also a function of these same variables. In addition, Negro employment will be influenced by any changes in the relative importance of each port since Negroes are in the majority of the longshore work force in some ports and in the minority in others.

Table 1 shows annual tonnage figures since the end of World War II for United States waterborne commerce. With some minor fluctuations, the total amount of cargo handled annually has grown steadily increasing from 767 million short tons in 1947 to 1,532 million short tons in 1970. The domestic portion, *i.e.* cargo shipped between two ports in the United States, accounted for about two-thirds of the total in 1970, a decrease from 75 percent in 1947. Foreign shipments, on the other hand, have grown at a rapid rate over the same period and are becoming increasingly more important.

These figures do not reflect substantially the actual amount of cargo handled by longshoremen. General cargo, which is the only cargo handled by longshoremen, makes up less than one-third of all United States waterborne commerce. Whereas, bulk cargo, which requires special loading and unloading equipment and is not handled by longshore crews, makes up the remaining two-thirds, with the crude oil and petroleum products imported from the oil-rich Middle East countries providing much of the foreign commerce.

As will be discussed later, technology has substantially reduced the amount of longshore labor required in the loading and unloading of general cargo. In particular, containerization has eliminated much of the work previously available to longshoremen by substituting capital for labor or by moving the loading of containers away from the docks. Despite the annual growth in waterborne commerce, the amount of work available to long-

TABLE 1. *Longshore Industry*
United States Waterborne Commerce [a]
1947-1970

Year	Total	Foreign	Domestic	Year	Total	Foreign	Domestic
1947	767	188	579	1959	1,054	326	727
1948	793	163	630	1960	1,100	339	761
1949	741	165	575	1961	1,062	329	733
1950	821	169	651	1962	1,129	359	771
1951	924	232	692	1963	1,174	386	788
1952	887	227	660	1964	1,238	422	816
1953	923	217	706	1965	1,273	444	829
1954	868	214	654	1966	1,334	471	863
1955	1,016	271	745	1967	1,337	466	871
1956	1,093	327	766	1968	1,396	508	888
1957	1,131	359	773	1969	1,449	521	927
1958	1,005	309	696	1970	1,532	581	951

Source: U.S. Bureau of the Census, *Statistical Abstract of the United States:*
1954: Table 693, p. 594.
1958: Table 751, p. 583.
1962: Table 809, p. 590.
1965: Table 843, p. 597.
1968: Table 867, p. 578.
1972: Table 941, p. 571.

[a] Millions of short tons (2,000 lbs.).

shoremen remained relatively stable before declining over the past decade. The advent of containerization and the decasualization of the longshore work force have had serious impacts on the job opportunities available to black and white longshoremen.

Longshoremen handle general cargo carried both by American and foreign-flag vessels. With American ships carrying only a small portion of our international commerce, foreign shipping plays an important part in providing work for the longshore industry. Nonetheless, coastwise shipments, which by law are reserved for American vessels, still make up about two-thirds of the total waterborne commerce making American shipping the largest customer of the longshore industry.

Major Ports of the United States

Table 2 gives the tonnage figures for waterborne commerce received or shipped by major ports in the United States during 1950, 1960, and 1970. The total tonnage handled in these ports is roughly one-half the total commerce of the United States as indicated in Table 1. As mentioned earlier, much of the waterborne commerce consists of bulk cargo, therefore, the figures in Table 2 tend to distort the relative importance of various port areas to the longshore industry. For example, the Great Lakes ports are important in terms of total commerce, although all but a small portion of the total tonnage handled in these ports is bulk cargo intended for industrial use. Consequently, these ports employ few longshoremen. It is, therefore, important to distinguish between the amounts of bulk and general cargo handled when discussing longshore activity as it relates to total waterborne commerce.

The longshore industry is concentrated in a relatively small number of ports. In terms of the amount of general cargo handled and the number of longshoremen employed, the Port of New York is the most important American port. New Orleans is the main Gulf port, and San Francisco is the leading port on the West Coast. The longshore forces in these and the other major ports will be discussed on an individual basis in later chapters. The concentration of the longshore industry, however, does have significance for Negro employment. Excluding the Great Lakes ports, Negroes are in a majority of the longshore work force in eight of the thirteen ports listed in Table 2. More important is that the job opportunities available to Negroes appear high, since a majority of the waterborne commerce mov-

TABLE 2. *Longshore Industry*
Waterborne Commerce by Major United States Ports[a]
1950, 1960, 1970

Port	1950	1960	1970
Atlantic Coast			
Boston, Mass.	17,645	17,996	25,032
Port of New York, N.Y.	86,603	101,626	111,947
Delaware River Ports	53,444	82,310	98,503
Baltimore, Md.	24,302	33,727	36,674
Norfolk, Hampton Roads, and Newport News, Va.	20,092	42,587	59,139
Gulf Coast			
Tampa, Fla.	6,504	12,544	29,797
New Orleans, La.	17,788	27,905	63,622
Houston, Tex.	27,778	36,820	39,443
Beaumont, Tex.	17,794	19,529	19,843
Port Arthur, Tex.	16,191	24,486	15,854
West Coast			
Long Beach, Calif.	5,004	8,932	21,035
Los Angeles, Calif.	19,282	21,807	21,652
San Francisco Bay Area, Calif.	24,098	34,330	39,651
Great Lakes			
Chicago, Ill.	19,906	20,714	26,890
Cleveland, Ohio	17,757	17,564	22,737
Detroit, Mich.	22,388	27,226	30,936
Duluth-Superior, Minn.	63,126	42,667	42,758
Toledo, Ohio	33,947	33,685	31,540

Source: U.S. Bureau of the Census, *Statistical Abstract of the United States:*
1952: Tables 652, 653, pp. 538-539.
1962: Tables 817, 818, pp. 595-596.
1972: Tables 949, 950, p. 574.

[a] Thousands of short tons (2,000 lbs.).

ing through those thirteen ports is handled in the ports containing the black longshore majority.

Nature of the Work

In essence, longshore work consists of loading and unloading ships, and has been further defined as "all handling of cargo in its transfer from vessel to first place of rest, and vice-versa, including sorting and piling of cargo from vessel to railroad car or barge, or vice-versa."[2] The entire cargo-handling operation is somewhat more complicated, however, and it is appropriate first to differentiate the various jobs performed by longshoremen from those done by other laborers working in the port area, and secondly to describe the job functions within the longshore gang. This can be accomplished by tracing the movement of cargo through the loading process. It should be noted, however, that the occupational structure in the industry varies somewhat from port to port.

Generally, cargo arrives on the pier by truck or by railroad car several days prior to its scheduled loading aboard ship. When the cargo is delivered to the terminal, it is separated, grouped, and stored in the marine terminal adjacent to the dock loading area. Once placed in temporary storage, the cargo is said to be in its "last place of rest." Up to this point, the work is generally performed by truck drivers, helpers, and warehousemen, although in some ports it is feasible for longshoremen to perform these functions.

Typically, longshore work begins with the movement of cargo from this "last place of rest," combining the efforts of three separate units of dock, deck, and hold gangs, which comprise the larger longshore gang. In the storage area ashore, dock workers place the cargo on pallets in preparation for loading. Tractor or forklift operators move these pallets from the warehouse to dock side and place them within reach of the ship's cargo handling gear. At this point, checkers, who are not part of the regular longshore gang, are assigned to check and record the cargo being loaded or unloaded. As will be noted later, the checker position historically has been closed to Negroes in most ports.

Cargo ships have several large hatches, which permits access to the ship's hold, and separate equipment for each hatch—usually masts and booms or a rotating crane. At dock side, frontmen or slingmen attach the hoisting gear to the cargo which was left near the ship's hold. In most ports, these functions are considered part of deck work, but on the West Coast, ship work begins with the attachment of the slings. Once aboard ship, the

2. Pacific Coast Longshore Agreement, 1956, as cited in Maritime Cargo Transportation Conference, *Longshore Safety Survey* (Washington: National Academy of Sciences, 1956), p. 13.

hoist is operated by a winch driver who transfers the cargo from the dock to the hold of the ship. Since his position at the controls does not allow him an unobstructed view of the cargo throughout the transfer operation, a hatch tender positions himself near the hatch opening and serves as the "eyes" of the winch operator as the cargo is lowered into the hold. The hatch tender uses hand signals to transmit instructions to the winch driver. Generally, the gang foreman serves as the hatch tender and directs the entire cargo loading operation. These two jobs of winch operator and hatch tender comprise the deck work and require special training and experience in the operation of the equipment. A distinguishing feature of Negro employment in the longshore industry is that there is a long history of Negro foremen. In some instances, Negroes have served as heads of "mixed" gangs, containing both Negroes and whites.

Inside the ship's hold, the hold gang receives the cargo, removes the sling, and moves the cargo to the wings of the hold where it is stowed for transport. The hold gang may also be responsible for the lashing and bracing of cargo in order to prevent damaging shifts during sea transportation. During loading operations, some of the more experienced men in the gang will be assigned to the hold since the placement of cargo is critical to the stability of the ship. Work in the hold of the ship is difficult, tiring, and unpleasant, and in some ports was often assigned to Negroes.

The less experienced men in the longshore gang are usually assigned to dock work. Mainly through experience and on-the-job training, they acquire the knowledge required for work in the hold and/or the skills necessary to operate the winch. Experience and specific skills, such as winch or crane operation, tend to create more job security for a longshoreman because dockworkers are generally not skilled.

The Gang Structure

One of the most important features of longshore work is the gang structure requiring the coordinated efforts of men working in the hold, on the deck, and on the dock. Gang members have always been required to work closely together for long and continuous periods of time. Since cargo handling requires a team effort and emphasis has always been placed upon fast ship turnaround time, employers are primarily interested in keeping the gangs intact throughout the job rather than hire others unfamiliar with the ship and the other members of the gang. On the other hand, because the longshoreman does not know when the next ship will arrive or if his gang will be chosen to work, he prefers to work as long as the job lasts with little regard for time off. The resulting system of work relationships and patterns benefits both the employer and the employees. For the longshoremen, the permanent gang system increases his job prospects and for the employers, it increases efficiency and safety.

In several of the major ports, gangs are hired rather than individual longshoremen. Usually, a gang boss or foreman, is selected for a job, and he either assembles his regular gang or chooses from among his following of longshoremen. In either case, the composition of the gang does not vary greatly from day to day. When a regular member of a gang is absent, the gang boss selects an "unattached" longshoreman to fill in on a temporary basis.

As Professor Northrup noted, ". . . working in gangs demands close comradeship and understanding, which appears to be more easily obtainable among homogeneous groups."[3] These homogeneous groups provided the cohesion necessary for the efficient operations of the gang, especially during periods of long and continuous work. Historically, the gangs have usually been made up of members of one ethnic or racial group,[4] although racially mixed gangs have been a feature of the New Orleans waterfront since 1937. As replacements were needed, the men were usually chosen from the same group to preserve the ethnic composition of the gang. Newly arrived immigrants became attracted to longshore work because of the minimal skill requirements and because they felt comfortable working with others of the same background already employed on the docks. Negroes also became attracted to longshore work finding employment with all-black gangs in most ports.

In contrast is the fact that an Irish gang would often work on the same pier as a German gang, but rarely would a gang consist of both German and Irish workers. All men in the labor force performed the same or similar tasks, but in most ports it was rare to find men of different nationalities or races working together out of the same hold. Although employees preferred

3. Herbert R. Northrup, *Organized Labor and the Negro* (New York: Kraus Reprint Co., 1971), pp. 142-143.

4. This phenomenon is discussed further in Chapter III.

working with persons of similar backgrounds, employers found it more efficient to use labor of one nationality or color.

UNIONIZATION

Unions have played a major role in the development of the longshore industry, and Negroes, in many cases, have been actively involved with the establishment of the union structure. This section attempts to present a brief overview of the historic development of the role of the longshoreman, the factors leading up to the organization of unions, and some of the major unions in each port.

Colonial Period to 1800

Since the colonial period, men have been employed on the docks of the Atlantic ports to load and unload the valuable cargo which was considered the supportive life-lines between the struggling new world and Europe. At first, ships arrived intermittently, but as commerce grew, the colonies became recognized as a potential world maritime and trading power. "By the time of the American Revolution stevedoring was one of the struggling nation's major fields of employment." [5]

The characteristics and nature of the longshoreman and his work has not changed substantially since those early days. "[L]ongshoring . . . ceased to be only the parttime occupation for men hastily called from their plows or blacksmith shops." [6] Gradually, skills based upon the various techniques necessary to stow the different types of cargo developed, and physical strength became the primary requirement for these men. The physical nature of their work, the long and erratic working hours, the physically poor conditions of both ship and dock, which were generally located in unsavory neighborhoods, weakened the reputation of these early longshoremen. Because of the "hurry up and wait" nature of the work, longshoremen were often found in dockside taverns waiting for work or their pay which were constantly in a state of flux.[7]

---

5. Maud Russell, *Men Along the Shore: The ILA and Its History* (New York: Brussel and Brussel, Inc., 1966), p. 8.

6. *Ibid.*

7. *Ibid.*, p. 9.

19th Century: Growth of the Unions

There is little doubt that during these early years of the new nation a "professional class" of longshoremen emerged, however, little information concerning their early development can be found. "Except when [longshoremen] struck little appeared in newspapers, diaries, or government records. This silence, this absence of the slightest interest in the men of the docks continued for two centuries."[8] But by the 1830's, dock workers began to realize their plight and began forming societies to help alleviate many of their problems.[9] It is most interesting to note the temper of this period of history. Russell writes that

> [i]t was a time of unrest—a period of great flexing of strength by the common people. President Andrew Jackson was in the last year of his "reign," which the conservatives of the time dubbed the rule of "King Mob." Such early reformers as Horace Mann and William Lloyd Garrison were agitating for change.[10]

Indeed, this era of discontent and social change affected the future of the longshore industry.

On the east coast this discontent over poor working conditions and fluctuating wages, reached strick proportions bringing the New York harbor to a near standstill and reaching riot proportions in Philadelphia. The longshoremen realized that in order to effectively fight against these conditions they must reorganize their groups and societies into unions.

Russell notes that the earliest waterfront unions were benevolent and social societies, organized for cultural and educational purposes, but also sought to increase the longshoremen's wages.[11] The earliest, viable organization of longshoremen was the Boston Longshoremen's Provident Union founded in 1847 by a state charter.[12] Barnes claims that this was originally ". . . a benevolent organization, but it gradually became a regular labor union, —the first longshore union in the country."[13]

---

8. *Ibid.*, p. 10.

9. *Ibid.*, p. 13.

10. *Ibid.*

11. *Ibid.*, p. 17.

12. Charles B. Barnes, *The Longshoremen* (New York: Russell Sage Foundation, 1915), p. 183.

13. *Ibid.*, p. 184.

By 1853 the Alongshoremen's United Benefit Society was founded in New York City. It too was initially a benevolent society but campaigned against low earnings and irregular employment. Typical of many organizations founded during this period, it did not survive, but rather gave way to the Alongshoremen's Union Protective Association in 1864. This association was later incorporated as the Longshoremen's Union Protective Association, No. 2 (LUPA) in 1866,[14] which was considered the first true union organized on economic grounds, "regulating the time and manner of employment."[15]

During this period, the South also witnessed the rise of similar organizations. Most 19th century longshore unions in these ports were composed primarily of Negroes. The Longshoremen's Protective Union Association, whose membership was entirely Negro, was organized in Charleston, South Carolina, in 1867 and in Port Royal, Georgia, in 1874.[16] The Charleston group was known then as "the most powerful organization of the colored laboring class in South Carolina."[17]

Gulf and West ports also saw the rise of union organizations. In 1850, the Screwmen's Benevolent Association was founded in New Orleans by those "who 'screwed' the cotton with hand screws and stowed it aboard ships."[18] "Enlistments in the Confederate Army during the Civil War so thinned the ranks of the Screwmen's Association that it was almost destroyed. However, it managed to survive and . . . to play a leading role on the New Orleans waterfront for more than seventy years."[19] Because of the difficulty of the work and the high level of skill required, the screwmen of New Orleans found themselves in a good bargaining position and received their wage demands without striking.

---

14. *Ibid.*, p. 95; and Charles P. Larrowe, *Shape-up and Hiring Hall* (Berkeley: University of California Press, 1955), p. 7.

15. *Ibid.*

16. Northrup, *op. cit.*, p. 147.

17. *Ibid.*

18. *Ibid.*, p. 149.

19. Herbert R. Northrup, "The New Orleans Longshoremen," *Political Science Quarterly*, Vol. LVII (December 1942), p. 527.

Negro longshoremen, in 1872, organized the Longshoremen's Protective Benevolent Association in order to cooperate with the all-white screwmen's union. One short year later, both white and black workers accused each other of monopolizing the longshore work, and as a result, "[t]he white screwmen sought to control the competition of the Negroes by assisting the colored men to form the Screwmen's Benevolent Association, No. I (colored), in 1875."[20]

The ports of Texas, Galveston and Houston in particular, have been organized for well over one hundred years. Following the lead of the New Orleans screwmen, the white cotton handlers in Galveston formed the Galveston Screwmen's Benevolent Association (GSBA) in 1866. Also fearing competition from the Negro, the GSBA resolved not to work for anyone who employed Negroes aboard ship.[21] The first Negro union in Galveston was, therefore, formed in 1870. Negro Longshoremen's Benevolent Association, which imitated the Galveston all-white association previously organized in 1869, restricted its members' work to the dock area.[22] The next decades saw white and black locals working rather peacefully under the work-sharing agreements.

Unions of the West Coast longshoremen existed almost as soon as the West Coast region was settled. There was a strike in 1851,[23] but as with the New York strike of 1836, records cannot be found of any formal organization. In 1853, the stevedore and ship-riggers in San Francisco founded the Riggers' and Stevedores' Union Association.[24] During the 1880's, the West Coast longshore industry organized the Longshore Lumberman's Protective Association and the Steamship Stevedores' Protective Union, which was formed to protect the rapidly increasing group of unskilled workers.[25]

---

20. *Ibid.*, p. 528.

21. F. Ray Marshall, *Labor in the South* (Cambridge: Harvard University Press, 1967), p. 65.

22. *Ibid.*

23. Betty V. H. Schneider and Abraham Siegel, *Industrial Relations in the Pacific Coast Longshore Industry* (Berkeley: Institute of Industrial Relations, University of California, 1956), p. 4.

24. *Ibid.*

25. *Ibid.*

The Knights of Labor

The Noble Order of the Knights of Labor was started by Uriah S. Stevens among the meat cutters of Philadelphia in 1869.[26] Stevens envisioned that workers should be "united not by common trades or crafts but by the mere fact that they were wage earners."[27] The "fraternity," created to organize, educate and direct "the power of the industrial masses," spread to all branches of labor and by December 1886 total membership was reported to be between 500,000 and 600,000.[28] Longshore branches of the Knights of Labor appeared in every major port city. The eastern ports were organized under District Assembly No. 49 in 1884, but because the assembly served all trades and crafts the waterfront members formed the Ocean Associations and the Maritime Associations.[29] Russell points out that

> [t]he first longshore Knights of Labor were men from the coastwise lines—a curious fact, for until that time there had been no organization whatever among these workers. All the union and protective associations previously described were exclusively for foreign commerce men. Coastwise dockers had always remained outside unionism; they were the lowest paid and most oppressed of all harbor employees.[30]

The Knights rapid success and growing popularity was further bolstered by the New York City streetcar strike in 1885. By 1885, the Knights of Labor phenominal and rapid growth resulted in over-organization.

> [t]he leaders felt constrained to check the initiation of new members. So huge and so sudden was the growth that they were inadequately prepared to handle the numerous labor disputes that arose among the many trades represented.[31]

This failure of the strike leadership affected the longshoremen in 1887. A disagreement which initially arose in the port of New York developed into the "Big Strike of 1887."[32] The strike

---

26. Russell, *op. cit.*, p. 31.

27. *Ibid.*

28. Barnes, *op. cit.*, p. 101.

29. Russell, *op. cit.*, p. 32.

30. *Ibid.*

31. Barnes, *op. cit.*, p. 102.

32. *Ibid.*, this strike will be discussed more fully in Chapter III, pp. 53-55.

produced tremendous solidarity among all port longshoremen, however, because of its length and the inadequate Knights leadership they lost all their demands—wages and all fringe benefits. This was a total disaster and dealt a final blow to unionism.[33] One year after the strike there were no longshore organizations left.[34]

20th Century and the ILA

Between 1886 and 1896 longshoremen were subjected to the mercy of shipowners.[35] The memory of the "Big Strike" ruined many attempts to reorganize the industry. In 1896, the Dockers' Union of England sent Edward McHugh to New York with the intention to organize all waterfront workers and seamen. Under the guidance of Bolton Hall, James R. Brown, Henry George, and McHugh the American Longshoremen's Union, known popularly as the McHugh Organization, was founded in 1896. The union achieved much during its short life. It restored the confidence of the longshoremen and secured better treatment from dock foremen. This lasted only a short time until Frank Devlin embezzled thousands of dollars, bankrupting the union and causing its ultimate downfall a mere two years after its organization.[36] The officials of the ALU quickly claimed bankruptcy thereby terminating the organization. They then formed another union under the old Longshoremen's Union Protective Association (LUPA) name, previously established in 1864.[37]

The International Longshoremen's Association, first organized in Chicago in 1877 by Dan Keefe, was formally named at the Detroit convention in 1892.[38] The ILA gradually extended its way from the Great Lakes down the East Coast, and then throughout the ports of the country. It affiliated with the AFL and, in turn, won affiliation from many of the local unions which had existed in the various ports for many years. It was greatly

33. *Ibid.*, p. 108.

34. Russell, *op. cit.*, p. 41.

35. Barnes, *op. cit.*, p. 108.

36. Russell, *op. cit.*, p. 51; and Barnes, *op. cit.*, p. 116.

37. *Ibid.*, pp. 113, 95.

38. Russell, *op. cit.*, pp. 61-62.

assisted in achieving hegemony during World War I when it was officially recognized by the United States government as an official spokesman for longshoremen. It took over rival groups in the Port of New York and elsewhere during this period. Also during World War I, longshoremen in New York, who have since that period always been the largest single local group within the ILA, achieved dominance in the organization and the top officers of the union ever since have been from that port.

The ILA has always admitted blacks without discrimination and it was one of the first unions to have a black vice president. On the other hand, the ILA has generally accepted the status quo affiliating separate unions of blacks and refusing to interfere with racial practices in any ports. The Port of New York, as well as in other ports, ethnic groups have also had locals confined exclusively, or almost exclusively, to that ethnic group.

The West Coast Situation

Although the ILA has continued to be the longshore union with the largest membership throughout this century, it lost its grip on the West Coast in the 1930's.

In 1898, most of the West Coast longshore unions affiliated with the ILA.[39] A long series of lost strikes, however, caused unionism to again virtually disappear from West Coast docks. During the strikes of 1901, 1916, and 1919, Negroes entered the port of San Francisco as strikebreakers.[40]

The strike of 1934 revived unionism and also witnessed the rise to power of Harry Bridges. One of Bridges' first actions was to insure that Negroes could gain entrance to the union—they were again used as strikebreakers in 1934 [41]—but several of his local unions continued to exclude blacks. Three years later, Bridges led the West Coast longshoremen out of the ILA to form the International Longshoremen's and Warehousemen's Union,[42] which first affiliated with the Congress of Industrial Organizations (CIO), and then in 1949, was disaffiliated from the CIO for communist domination. The union is still an independent and still run by Harry Bridges.

39. *Ibid.*

40. Northrup, *Organized Labor and the Negro, op. cit.*, p. 152.

41. *Ibid.*, p. 153.

42. *Ibid.*, p. 152.

The Shape-up and Union Corruption

Although the ILA survived to become one of the strongest unions in the country, it was not without racketeering and corruption. Some of the fault can be traced to the ILA in New York in 1916 when the first port-wide agreement was negotiated. This agreement contained provisions for wage increases and hiring preferences for union members, but it was silent on the need to limit the supply of labor and the need to regularize employment. This inaction may have planted the seeds of the corruption, which later grew within the union, since improved wages attracted a greater number of casual workers to the industry, with no corresponding increase in job opportunities.

Primary responsibility, particularly in New York, can be attributed to the prevalent hiring method known as the "shape-up." This system required that longshoremen assemble in a sort of half-circle in front of the pier where they hoped to find work. The hiring boss, walking among them, would choose those men who would be hired for the current work shift. This process would be repeated at each pier in the port, at least twice daily and often at concurrent times. According to Northrup, ". . . [the shape-up] gives the stevedore or hiring foreman tremendous power over the employment opportunities of longshoremen, with the consequence that job-selling and bribery and corruption of all sorts become quite common."[43] In addition to increases in the wages of longshoremen, the only significant gain registered by the ILA during the period 1916-1946 was a setting of three fixed times for daily shape-up.[44] Previously, a shape-up could be held at any time of the day requiring longshoremen to spend many idle hours near the piers waiting for work. By fixing the times of the shape-ups, the ILA eliminated this problem; however, it preserved the hiring procedure which spawned the corruption.

Unchecked, corruption seems to breed more corruption. In the 1930's, and quite possibly earlier, the ILA was infiltrated by gangsters and ex-convicts.[45] Joseph Ryan, who succeeded to the ILA presidency after Anthony Chlopek retired in 1927, was elected to a life term as president in 1943. Because he also served

---

43. *Ibid.*, pp. 139-140.

44. Larrowe, *op. cit.*, p. 15.

45. *Ibid.*, p. 20.

on the New York State Parole Board, he was in a position to funnell ex-convicts into the industry. The union leadership proved reluctant to institute any reforms; therefore, it could be concluded that these leaders were profiting for the corruption.

Finally, in 1952 in response to allegations of corruption in the ILA dating as far back as 1914, Governor Thomas E. Dewey of New York ". . . instructed the New York State Crime Commission to make a thorough investigation of waterfront crime, with special emphasis on the relationship between the shape-up, racketeering, and diversion of cargo from the port."[46] The commission found the union steeped in crime and corruption and suggested basic reforms designed to abolish the shape-up, which was felt to be the heart of the problem. It is also important to note that the commission heard considerable evidence that blacks were especially victimized by the situation at several New York City locations. The final report produced remarkably speedy action by the New York and New Jersey state legislatures and the U. S. Congress, with the recommendations becoming law in less than three months.[47]

In due course, the shape-up was replaced with employment centers operated by the Bi-State Waterfront Commission, a government agency jointly operated by New York and New Jersey to police the Port of New York. The new hiring procedure and its decasualizing effect on the labor force are discussed more fully under the heading "Decasualization" in this chapter. Interestingly enough, New Orleans, which remained a casual port during this period, was relatively crime free.

Embarassed by the crime commission's findings, AFL President George Meany issued an ultimatum to Ryan to either eliminate the criminal element in the ILA or face the association's expulsion from the AFL. Following Ryan's failure to institute effective reforms, the AFL finally expelled the union in September 1953, and set up its own rival union, but the ILA won the representation elections conducted by the NLRB in 1954. Immediately following this defeat, the AFL gave up any further organizing efforts in the Port of New York. Five years later, in 1959, the ILA reaffiliated with the AFL-CIO. Although the ILA still had not met the requirements for reinstatement set down in 1953, the possibility of the ILA joining the Teamsters appar-

46. *Ibid.*, p. 41.

47. *Ibid.*, pp. 44-45.

ently caused the AFL-CIO to waive some of the requirements. Ryan, in the meantime, had retired.

DECASUALIZATION

In terms of strengthening the attachment of men to the longshore industry, the most important development has been the decasualization of the major ports. Decasualization can be described as the process whereby an oversupply of labor to an industry is reduced so that those remaining will have a more stable employment pattern and higher total earnings. In the longshore industry, the basic institution through which the decasualization process has been achieved is the central hiring hall. It is important to note that decasualization is responsible for a large decrease in the longshore work force. Concomitantly, decasualization is responsible for a decrease in the number of jobs available to black longshoremen. The data to be presented in later chapters, however, indicate that decasualization did not cause any changes in the relative position of Negro and white longshoremen. In other words, there were no significant shifts in the black percentage of total employment in any of the ports that were attributable to decasualization.

The general history of the longshore industry can be divided into two periods: one preceding decasualization and one beginning with decasualization. The process, however, did not occur at the same time nor to the same extent in each port. For example, Seattle became the first major port to decasualize when employers established a central hiring hall in 1921. On the other hand, the Port of New York, the largest in the country, did not attempt decasualization until 1953, doing so only after the New York State Crime Commission investigations and recommendations were presented. Although each port is unique in the way it has formalized the hiring process, the general characteristics of the change have been similar.

The Casual Port

Prior to decasualization, the longshore industry had all the main elements conducive to a casual labor market: the demand for labor varies from day to day, depending upon the number of ships in port at a given time. Furthermore, the demand is highly unpredictable and cannot be forecast more than a day or two in advance.

> In addition to . . . irregularity in the arrival and departure of ships, the shipping industry as a whole is seriously affected by cyclical trends, by seasonal fluctuations, by changes in tariff regulations, by the weather, and by the vagaries of the individual shipping companies. As a result it is wellnigh impossible to plan or gage the demand for longshore labor in the port for any considerable period of time.[48]

The industry is also characterized by a large number of employers each interested in maintaining a labor supply large enough to meet peak demands, which may be three times as great as normal demand.

Many longshoremen maintained a tenuous attachment to the industry since the work was usually of short duration and few of the employers provided permanent jobs. There is some evidence to indicate that in some ports, Negroes comprised a greater percentage of the casual work force than of the "permanently attached" work force.

Longshore work, albeit hard labor, never required special skills; therefore, anyone with a strong back could enter the work force. Consequently, in addition to the workers who earned their livelihoods as longshoremen, the waterfront attracted many men who were looking only for a few hours of employment. The net effects of having a casual labor force were that, on the average, many more men were attached to the industry than were needed, few achieved more than a subsistence earnings level, and the power to hire or not to hire rested in the hands of the hiring foremen.

As noted earlier, the shape-up, common in most ports prior to 1950, required that men looking for work line up at the base of the pier in hopes the hiring foreman would select them when work became available.

> The contracting stevedores doing the work of discharging and loading ships are seldom in a position to know in advance how long the actual work of loading or discharging will last and how many men they will need for this work. Hence there has developed a system of hiring longshoremen by the hour and hiring them only when and where actually needed. Every pier in port, every dock, becomes a hiring station, and the average longshoreman never knows whether or not he will be employed at a given pier or when hired how long he will remain on the job.[49]

A longshoreman seeking work on the waterfront is often forced to spend many idle hours not far from the docks. If he is not

48. "Employment Conditions and Unemployment Relief," *Monthly Labor Review*, Vol. XXXVII (December 1933), p. 1300.

49. *Ibid.*

chosen during the first shape-up he must "wait around" for a ship to arrive since prior notice of arrivals was not available.

> There is required at all times a great deal of hanging about awaiting the arrival of ships or frieght. This is a matter not of minutes but of hours; sometimes of whole days. Longshoremen, except while at work, are not allowed on the piers. They can not go to their homes for fear they will not be on hand when wanted. Consequently, they must stand on the sidewalks, in doorways, or on street corners. . . .[50]

From the employers point of view, the pool of idle men create the large supply of labor needed to meet peak demands when many ships were in port and had to be loaded and/or unloaded as fast as possible, and the shape-up created a total supply far in excess of what was needed on any particular day. In addition, it also created shortages on some piers and oversupplies on others with no means of matching supply and demand throughout the port area. To be sure, employers rarely needed as many men as were "attached" to a pier, but in the event the need arose, suitable labor was available. As will be discussed below, the shape-up allowed hiring foremen to exercise an extreme amount of power over the lines of longshoremen. In many instances, this power was manifested in the exclusion of Negroes. Having an oversupply of labor also made it easier to recruit strikebreakers, and blacks often served in this capacity.

> The supply side of the labor market is usually glut. The work is essentially unskilled. The extremely high turnover—perhaps 50 percent per day—is evidence of the large amount of daily hiring. Large numbers of unemployed or casually employed persons capable of doing the work are attracted by the reasonable probability of a job, however brief. Occasional success in actually getting a job strengthens the attachment to the industry of even the grossly underemployed. The employers collectively are interested in maintaining a labor force at least sufficient to meet peak period demand, but this interest usually requires little more than hiring the fringe worker just often enough to keep him coming to the docks.[51]

One of the factors that attracted fringe workers to the waterfront was the possibility of a few days of work and then a few days off. This type of employment had particular appeal for men who were not interested in a steadier job. The industry also offered part-time employment to those out of work elsewhere,

---

50. Barnes, *op. cit.*, p. 18.

51. Hartman, *op. cit.*, p. 26.

perhaps on lay-off or strike. In short, the hard work of longshoring was suited to those not capable of steady employment elsewhere.

The Effects of Decasualization

With the introduction of new technology in cargo handling, the manpower requirements of the industry decreased. In order to prevent fringe workers from siphoning off employment opportunities and income from the basic work force and also to insure the hiring of experienced men, employers and unions in the major ports developed methods whereby longshoremen were to be hired from central hiring halls. Longshoremen were required to register with the hall in order to become eligible for employment. Furthermore, longshoremen were requird to work a minimum number of hours per month to avoid being dropped from the register.

> Decasualization schemes . . . concentrate on manipulating the longshore labor supply in an effort to adjust the supply to the changing demands of the shipping industry. The employer has to relinquish the right to hire longshoremen from anywhere but the central office, where the register of longshoremen is kept. . . .
>
> A decasualization program has the effect of eliminating the power of the hiring agent, as well as the abuses and the nepotism that generally accompany it. It gradually reduces the total number of longshoremen in a port to a level that is close to the needs of the market. One result is that average earnings are raised for those men who are left in the the register.[52]

The basic work force is generally defined as those longshoremen who work a minimum of 700 to 800 hours per year. This minimum is usually the number of hours required to qualify for union pension benefits. Using this minimum, a 1964 study of ten Atlantic and Gulf Coast ports conducted by the U.S. Department of Labor indicated that, in the majority of the casual ports, less than one-half of the men hired during the previous year worked more than the minimum number of hours.[53] In contrast, the study also showed that in the Port of New York, which has been

---

52. Hosseine Morewedge, *The Economics of Casual Labor: A Study of the Longshore Industry* (Berne, Switzerland: Herbert Lang & Co., Ltd., 1970), p. 113.

53. U.S. Department of Labor, *Manpower Utilization-Job Security in the Longshore Industry: Boston* (Washington: U.S. Department of Labor, 1964), pp. 9-10.

decasualized since 1953, over four-fifths of the longshoremen worked more than 700 hours per year.[54] As a result of decasualization, however, the number of longshoremen in the Port of New York declined from 50,000 in 1953 to 23,000 in 1967.[55] With a reduction in the number of "part-time" longshoremen has come a rise in the income level and increased employment opportunities for those remaining in the industry. Most important, however, is that many of the evils attendant to the shape-up have been removed through the use of hiring halls.

The effects of decasualization upon Negroes varies from port to port. In southern ports, Negroes continued to maintain their numerical majority; however, in northern and eastern ports charges of discrimination continued to be brought against the ILA.[56] These charges stemmed from the days of the shape-up when hiring was strictly controlled by foremen and exclusion was a common practice. Although hiring was taken out of the hands of foremen, most gangs remained intact and working relationships continued to operate, excluding Negroes from many longshore jobs. In 1959, the Urban League of Greater New York charged that "the only Negroes with relatively permanent employment on the waterfront were in gangs performing the most 'arduous and least desirable work.' "[57] In addition, the League noted that "[h]undreds of casual longshoremen were hired, but Negro longshoremen were repeatedly ignored during the shape-up."[58] It is apparent that racial problems were not solved and that racial employment patterns were substantially unaltered by the advent of decasualization.

54. *Ibid.*

55. Joseph P. Goldberg, "Modernization in the Maritime Industry: Labor-Management Adjustments to Technological Change," in Harold Levinson *et al., Collective Bargaining and Technological Change in American Transportation* (Evanston, Ill.: Transportation Center, Northwestern University. 1971), p. 264.

56. Ray Marshall, *The Negro and Organized Labor* (New York: John Wiley and Sons, Inc., 1965), pp. 286-289.

57. *Ibid.*, p. 287.

58. *Ibid.*

PRODUCTIVITY AND TECHNOLOGICAL CHANGE

The nature of longshore work has changed little since colonial times. Until the recent introduction of containerization, the longshore industry has been slow to make any changes designed to improve productivity. The reluctance on the part of employers to make use of new cargo-handling methods stems from a lack of sufficient economic incentive. Furthermore, strong forces, including the longshore unions, have a vested interest in preserving the labor intensity of the industry and have traditionally opposed any technological changes which would reduce the size of the labor input. Any proposed changes in cargo handling would place the employer in direct conflict with the union.

Essentially, stevedores bill ship operators on a "cost plus" basis. The stevedores submit estimates based on the productivity of longshoremen, their wages, and any penalty fees to be paid to workers for handling certain cargoes. Overhead, insurance, and profits comprise the remainder of the estimate. In 1955, the Pacific Maritime Association estimated profits at 30 percent of straight-time wages and 10 percent of overtime wages.[59] If, for some reason, the estimate falls short of the actual cost, the ship operator generally pays the difference. For example, a union negotiated wage increase automatically raises an estimate. Since the stevedore still receives his profit, he is under no economic pressure to cut costs.

As noted earlier, stevedoring firms tend to be highly competitive, exhibit little differences between estimates submitted by different firms for the same contract, and incur man-hour labor costs that do not vary from firm to firm since contract negotiations between the employers and the longshore union set wage rates and penalty fees that apply to all firms throughout a given port area. Productivity, therefore, is also uniform because longshoremen are hired through a central union hiring hall on a rotating basis. Individual employers generally do not have permanent work crews and will employ a different longshore gang for each contract. Consequently, over a long period of time, productivity will be the same for all employers. Competition in the industry eliminates excess profits but still allows each firm a fair return.

---

59. U.S. Congress, House, Committee on Merchant Marine and Fisheries, *Study of Harbor Conditions in Los Angeles and Long Beach, Hearings* (October 19-21, 1955), 84th Cong., 1st sess. (Washington, 1955), pp. 101-102, as cited in Hartman, *op. cit.*, p. 13.

An additional factor limiting the introduction of new technology is that few stevedores own marine terminal facilities. Generally, the facilities are government-owned with stevedores supplying only the cargo handling services. Since they do not own the facilities, stevedores cannot be expected to make any of the major capital improvements that are necessary for increased productivity.

However, the largest obstacle to technological change has been union resistance. Since increased productivity is usually associated with fewer jobs or fewer man-hours per job, technological innovation threatens the job security of union members. To preserve the number of jobs available to its members, the unions have opposed any change that substitutes capital for labor. In most cases, the stevedoring firms have been too small or too fragmented to fight successfully the union on this issue.

Most of the improvements introduced to the industry have come from the initiative of the larger steamship lines that provide their own cargo handling services. The impetus for innovation stems from increasing competition from foreign operators that forced American carriers to search for ways to reduce costs. Since cargo handling costs account for almost one-half of total freight costs,[60] they became the prime target for reductions resulting in new cargo-handling methods that increased productivity and, at the same time, reduced labor requirements. These new methods allowed the steamship lines to realize additional savings as a result of faster ship turnaround time; however, they reduced the job opportunities available to Negro and white longshoremen.

The large shipping lines are in a better position to innovate for several reasons. First, they maintain their own marine terminal facilities and can make major capital improvements. Secondly, the larger lines can obtain the financing necessary for large capital expenditures and for new cargo handling equipment. Thirdly, by providing cargo handling services for their own ships, these lines can realize large cost savings through greater utilization of new equipment; and finally, the steamship lines are better able to withstand union opposition. Interestingly, the successful introduction of new cargo-handling methods by the larger steamship lines have usually been followed by similar improvements made in government-owned facilities.

---

60. Organization for Economic Co-operation and Development, *Ocean Freight Rates as Part of Total Costs, 1968,* as cited in Goldberg, *op. cit.*, p. 261.

Innovations

Until recently, the tools of the trade for a longshoreman were a strong back and a "cotton hook," the symbol of longshore work. Even as late as the 1930's, longshoremen relied on their muscle to get the job done. Cargo was transferred between the hold of a ship and dock on lift boards or sling boards that were nothing more than wide planks used in conjunction with rope slings. In the late 1930's and during World War II, pallets, which are raised wooden platforms, came into widespread use. Once loaded on a pallet, cargo may be moved within the ship, transferred to the dock, and warehoused as a single unit. This relatively simple innovation was instrumental in substituting machine power for muscle power in longshore work.

Containerization simply extended the concept of a unit load to larger units. Nonetheless, it represented a major technological innovation for the industry, impacting upon every facet of longshoring including manpower. As originally conceived, the containers were metal boxes of varying proportions, superseded in the mid-1950's by larger containers which could be transferred directly between ship and either truck or railroad car. Developed by Sea Train, Sea-Land, and Matson containerization successfully substituted capital for labor, both Negro and white, in cargo-handling operations and greatly increased productivity. "With 20 to 25 tons loaded by container in 2½ minutes, as against 18 to 20 manhours required for break-bulk handling, increased output per manhour was early projected at least in the range of 13 to 18 times, with further gains from faster ship turnaround in port."[61] From the point of view of the steamship companies, the only drawback to containerization was the substantial capital outlay for specialized handling equipment and the containers themselves.

The impact of containerization extends in many directions. In addition to savings in freight costs that accrue as a result of reduced handling, reduced turnaround time in port for a ship means faster shipment and, therefore, more voyages per ship. The use of containers reduces packaging costs, pilferage costs, and damage to the goods during shipment. The popularity of this concept has virtually revolutionized the shipping business.

61. Goldberg, *op. cit.*, p. 269.

Containerization has had other revolutionary effects on the longshore industry. Most important is that the role of the longshoreman has shifted from handling palletized cargo to operating the crane that lifts the containers. In addition to the crane operator, the only labor required in the operation is a man to attach the slings and a man to remove the slings and secure the container to its new platform. This reduction in the amount of labor required has had a strong impact on the industry's employment and continues to reduce the number of jobs available for longshoremen.

An interesting aspect of containerization in the Port of New York has been its beneficial impact on black employment. Containerization had led to a transfer of work and a shift of jobs from Manhattan to Newark and Elizabeth, New Jersey, primarily because of the need for space for trucks and containers. In this New Jersey area, large numbers of blacks live and find employment; in Manhattan, the longshore labor force has been overwhelmingly white. This is thus one of the few occasions where shifts of employment because of technological change has benefited blacks.

Union Response to Innovation

Technology, in the form of handling equipment and ship design, continually reduces the number of men required to work a particular ship, but the unions, to a large extent, have always been able to mitigate the detrimental effects. For example, the cotton screwmen of the South continued to enjoy high wages, steady employment, and almost complete job control for many years after the high density cotton press was invented and introduced on the waterfront. The existence of the cotton press rendered obsolete the screwmens' specialized skill, but strong union organization helped the screwmen maintain job control in New Orleans and the Texas ports. The development of pallets and palletized cargoes during World War II did little to reduce the size of longshore gangs since bargaining power greatly favored the union. In the 1960's, containerization was countered by negotiated royalty payments to the union for each container handled and a negotiated right, under certain conditions, to pack or re-pack containers at dockside.

Under pressure for increased productivity, however, industry employment has, in fact, declined and job functions have changed, but the longshore unions have coped with this problem of change in various ways. For example, on the West Coast, the International Longshoremen's and Warehousemen's Union (ILWU) anticipated the need for change, and through negotiations with employers, sought to soften the impact of this change in the work force. In contrast, however, the ILA attempted to deal with the problem only after it could no longer be ignored.

SUMMARY

There are a few factors concerning the nature and structure of the industry and the longshoremen themselves that become apparent. First, the work has been and, to a large degree, still is unskilled labor; however, to those employed in longshoring, it was the only work available and therefore worth protecting. As will be noted in the next chapter, the protection took the form of exclusion of other people not sharing in the dominant nationality or color on the pier in question. Fierce competition between Irish and Italians or Irish and Negro, often in the form of violent attack, has been an integral part of the history of the waterfront. Negroes, however, have always worked in the industry either as strikebreakers—later permanent waterfront workers—in the Northeast and on the West Coast, or as original longshoremen and union members in the South and along the Gulf Coast.

On the West Coast the ILWU negotiated a contract permitting the introduction of labor saving machinery in return for a substantial benefit package. The so-called mechanization and modernization agreement resulted in a substantial improvement in productivity which came at a time of the expansion of these ports partly attributable to the Vietnam war. This expansion greatly increased employment opportunities including those for Negroes.[62]

On the East Coast, however, a series of strikes erupted as the union fought technological change, but they gradually reduced and improved methods accepted. Here again mechanization did not cause any special adverse effect on blacks particularly because of the fact that expansion occurred in the Port of New York on the New Jersey side where a larger percentage of blacks worked, and contraction occurred primarily in the Manhattan area which was largely white. Contraction was particularly strong in the

62. Hartman, *op. cit.*, pp. 81-82.

passenger ship berths along Manhattan as the jet powered air plane took over the work formerly done by the large passenger ships.

Negroes have not suffered disproportionately in this decline. Important also is that manpower requirements have diminished greatly over the years. The primary causes of the decrease in longshore job opportunities have been the effects of decasualization, which removed the large number of casual workers who were perpherally tied to the industry, and the introduction of such advances as containerization, which reduced the number of men necessary to load and unload the ships.

Unionism in longshoring predates organization in most other segments of the economy. Although there were many organizations on the waterfront in the 1800's, most organized longshoremen came under the International Longshoremen's Association (ILA) by World War I or shortly thereafter. The racial policies of the ILA were not at all typical of early unions in the United States. In the 1940's, Northrup wrote:

> From its inception in 1892, the ILA has officially opposed racial discrimination. Negroes compose a large portion of its membership, and today four of its fifteen vice-presidents are colored. No less an authority than William Green, president of the AFL, has declared that the ILA applies the Federation's "cardinal principle" of non-discrimination "more religiously" than any of its other affiliates. Actually, however, Negro-union relations vary considerably from port to port. In many instances, strong local unions had been in existence for years before they affiliated with the ILA, and their racial policies were developed without regard to those of the national union.[63]

The most important function of the union, however, is that the hiring process is under its close control. Although the shape-up has been eliminated for the most part, the hiring halls and the dispatchers are administered entirely by either the union or the union in joint cooperation with the employers. This procedure is present in all major ports except New Orleans where the hiring hall is employer controlled. The longshore industry, even in New Orleans, operates under an arrangement which guarantees that only union members will become permanently attached to the waterfront work force.

It is important to reemphasize that the union structure in the longshore industry has allowed for the development of a strong cadre of black union officials who exercise more influence over the economic well-being of their constituents, and themselves, than can be found in any other industry.

---

63. Northrup, *Organized Labor and the Negro, op. cit.*, p. 141.

CHAPTER III

The Negro Struggle for Waterfront Jobs

In the South Atlantic and Gulf ports, Negroes have always performed longshore work. Slaves loaded the tobacco barrels and cotton bales, and after the Civil War blacks continued to dominate the work. Relatively high wage rates and the need for special skills in loading materials, especially before mechanical contrivances were developed, brought whites to the job in some ports also. There resulted a system of separate gangs by race and thence in some ports, separate union locals. Although these locals divided the work, whites often received a larger share of the jobs than blacks and the latter were assigned less favorable work.

In the Northeast, longshore work became the province of the various ethnic groups who came to this country in the great immigration waves. Negroes in many cases won longshore work only after being utilized as strikebreakers, however, blacks in the South were early participants in both the formation of unions and in strikes. In the North, also, sections of ports and types of work were frequently controlled by one ethnic group, and gangs are still often composed of a single ethnic strain or race.

On the West Coast, few blacks found their way to dock work until the 1930's, and even as late as 1960, Portland, Oregon, and Los Angeles/Long Beach, California, dockworkers excluded Negroes from their midst. In disregard of a union policy favorable to integration, this discriminatory treatment was not ended until after the passage of the Civil Rights Act of 1964.

Despite the long history of black employment in the industry, the job of checker in all ports has remained a white man's preserve. Even today, only a few blacks enjoy this semi-white collar position. This chapter will look at black employment in the nation's principal ports, treating each port as a separate entity, after first examining overall national and regional employment trends.

TABLE 3. *Longshore Industry*
Total and Negro Employment[a] *by Region*
1910-1970

Region	1910			1920			1930		
	Total	Negro	Percent Negro	Total	Negro	Percent Negro	Total	Negro	Percent Negro
Total United States	62,813	16,379	26.1	85,605	27,206	31.8	73,944	25,434	34.4
Northeast (4)	30,392	2,837	9.3	49,570	8,496	17.1	33,990	6,406	18.8
South Atlantic (5)	10,462	8,938	85.4	13,311	11,595	87.1	10,109[b]	8,700	86.1
South Central (3)	5,928	3,146	53.1	9,108	5,924	65.0	10,691	8,075	75.5
North Central (2)	2,239	229	10.2	n.a.	n.a.	—	705	n.a.	—
West (1)	2,593	38	1.5	3,728	44	1.2	6,346	91	1.4

Region	1940			1950		
	Total	Negro	Percent Negro	Total	Negro	Percent Negro
Total United States	63,241	20,279	32.1	62,003	21,197	34.2
Northeast (4)	25,552	3,486	13.6	26,707	4,740	17.7
South Atlantic (5)	10,879	9,077	83.4	7,938	6,367	80.2
South Central (3)	9,539	6,682	70.0	10,026	6,912	68.9
North Central (2)	1,443	104	7.2	1,080	170	15.7
West (1)	6,865	83	1.2	8,481	2,032	24.0

Region	1960			1970		
	Total	Negro	Percent Negro	Total	Negro	Percent Negro
Total United States	55,479	19,129	34.5	42,349	15,326	36.2
Northeast (4)	20,640	3,596	17.4	12,530	2,606	20.8
South Atlantic (5)	6,495	5,118	78.8	5,886	4,325	73.5
South Central (3)	10,417	7,105	68.2	8,508	5,018	59.0
North Central (2)	939	385	41.0	978	434	44.4
West (1)	7,869	1,820	23.1	6,276	1,636	26.1

Source: *U.S. Census of Population:*
1910: Vol. IV, *Occupational Statistics*, Tables 6, 7.
1920: Vol. IV, *Occupations*, Table 1, pp. 875-1033; Table 6, p. 386; Table 10, p. 427.
1930: Vol. IV, *Occupations, by States*, Tables 4, 11, 13.
1940: Vol. III, *The Labor Force*, Part 1, U.S. Summary, Table 60, Part 2, Table 13.
1950: Vol. II, *Characteristics of the Population*, Part 1, U.S. Summary, Table 128, State Volumes, Table 77.
1960: Vol. I, *Characteristics of the Population*, Part 1, U.S. Summary, Table 205, State Volumes, Table 122.
1970: PC(1)-D, *Detailed Characteristics*, U.S. Summary, Table 223, State Volumes, Table 171.

Note: Totals do not equal sum of entries due to the exclusion of all but 15 states.

[a] Figures for male employees only.

[b] Contains 4 states only; South Carolina not available for Negroes, excludes 963 total males.

Regional definitions:
Northeast: Massachusetts, New Jersey, New York, Pennsylvania.
South Atlantic: Georgia, Florida, Maryland, South Carolina, Virginia.
South Central: Alabama, Louisiana, Texas.
North Central: Illinois, Michigan.
West: California.

Tables 3 and 4 present a geographical breakdown of longshore employment from 1910 to 1970[64] and serve as the background for the port-by-port analysis which follows. As can be seen in Tables 3 and 4, blacks comprised approximately two-thirds to three-quarters of the work force in the southern regions over the 1910-1970 period.[65] In the Northeast, the black participation rate increased from 9.3 percent in 1910 to 17.4 percent in 1960 and then to 20.8 percent in 1970. The most significant increase, however, considering both absolute and percentage increases, occurred in California where blacks made considerable advances between 1940 and 1970. Some of this increase could be attributed to the fact that California is the only state to experience a 200 percent increase in total longshore employment over the time span covered by Tables 3 and 4. On a national level, the percent Negro data reflect the highest percentages found in any industry in the country for the same time period except in the case of the tobacco industry for the pre-1970 period, and that industry is concentrated in three southern states.

Table 4 presents the same data as Table 3 but distributed by geographical area and employment concentration. The differences between concentrations of total employment and black employment are rather clear. In the 1910-1930 period, approximately 51.2 percent of total employment was concentrated in the Northeast and a varying percentage of Negro employment, never reaching one-third, was so situated. The exact opposite is true when considering the two southern regions as one over the same period. In the South, total employment never reached 30 percent of all those employed in longshoring, and Negro employment never fell below 64 percent of all Negroes in the industry. The historical use of Negro slaves on southern docks, coupled with the concentrations of Negro population there account for the heavy black southern percentages.[66]

In the 1940-1970 period, it is apparent that blacks became more involved in longshoring in New York, New Jersey, and California. The geographic concentrations of employment were altered somewhat, the Northeast accounted for a decreasing pro-

64. Adequate census data for the pre-1910 period are unavailable.

65. Combining the two southern regions in Table 3, the participation rates are 73.7 percent, 78.1 percent, 80.6 percent, 77.2 percent, 73.9 percent, and 72.3 percent for census years 1910 through 1960.

66. These statements are verified in later sections.

portion of total and black employment whereas the West Coast accounted for a large increase in both. In addition, the South Central region also showed an increase in the proportions of total and black employment centered there. This region includes the port of New Orleans, the second busiest port in the nation, and the ports of Texas including Houston, a great expanding center of commerce.

On a region-by-region basis, the data point out some interesting shifts in the longshore work force. In the Northeast, the total work force declined approximately 32.1 percent between 1910 and 1960: the decrease was 58.8 percent considering the 1910-1970 period and the decasualization occurring in the 1960's. Negro employment, however, increased approximately 21.1 percent between 1910-1960 and decreased only 8.1 percent over the entire 1910-1970 period. The largest gains were recorded in the 1910-1920 period as total employment increased approximately 63.1 percent and Negro employment increased almost 200 percent, however, both groups experienced continued declines in employment through 1960. The net result was an increase in black participation in Northeast longshoring. The 1910-1920 increase in Negro representation corresponds to the information presented later which indicates that Negroes gained permanent entrance into the industry during this period. Of course, the 1910-1920 period includes World War I when shipping from the Port of New York reached record levels and manpower shortages on the docks were common. These data show that decasualization increased the proportion of blacks working in the Northeast longshore industry.

A similar movement in total employment can be observed for the South Atlantic region between 1910 and 1970. Total employment decreased approximately 43.6 percent, but Negro employment decreased only 51.6 percent during this period. The obvious conclusion is that whites were gaining more longshore jobs in South Atlantic ports during the period, although in 1970 almost three of every four longshore positions were filled by Negroes. Important also is that the relative share of total and Negro longshore employment in this region declined between 1910 and 1970. Significant, in terms of the concentration of the Negro longshore work force, is that in 1910, 54.6 percent of all Negro longshoremen worked on South Atlantic docks; however, by 1970, the percentage had decreased to 28.2 percent. These data indicate the relative decline in the importance of South Atlantic ports.

TABLE 4. *Longshore Industry*
Percent Distribution of Total and Negro Employment by Region
Selected States, 1910-1970

Region	1910				1920				1930			
	Total	Percent	Negro	Percent	Total	Percent	Negro	Percent	Total	Percent	Negro	Percent
Total United States	62,813	100.0	16,379	100.0	85,605	100.0	27,206	100.0	73,944	100.0	25,434	100.0
Northeast (4)	30,392	48.4	2,837	17.3	49,570	57.9	8,496	31.2	33,990	46.0	6,406	25.2
South Atlantic (5)	10,462	16.7	8,938	54.6	13,311	15.5	11,595	42.6	11,072	15.0	8,700	34.2
South Central (3)	5,928	9.4	3,146	19.2	9,108	10.6	5,924	21.8	10,691	14.5	8,075	31.7
North Central (2)	2,239	3.6	229	1.4	n.a.	—	n.a.	—	705	1.0	n.a.	—
West (1)	2,593	4.1	38	0.2	3,728	4.4	44	0.2	6,346	8.6	91	0.4

Region	1940				1950			
	Total	Percent	Negro	Percent	Total	Percent	Negro	Percent
Total United States	63,241	100.0	20,279	100.0	62,003	100.0	21,197	100.0
Northeast (4)	25,552	40.4	3,486	17.2	26,707	43.1	4,740	22.4
South Atlantic (5)	10,879	17.2	9,077	44.8	7,938	12.8	6,367	30.0
South Central (3)	9,539	15.1	6,682	33.0	10,026	16.2	6,912	32.6
North Central (2)	1,443	2.3	104	0.5	1,080	1.7	170	0.8
West (1)	6,865	10.9	83	0.4	8,481	13.7	2,032	9.6

Region	1960				1970			
	Total	Percent	Negro	Percent	Total	Percent	Negro	Percent
Total United States	55,479	100.0	19,129	100.0	42,349	100.0	15,326	100.0
Northeast (4)	20,640	37.2	3,596	18.8	12,530	29.6	2,606	17.0
South Atlantic (5)	6,495	11.7	5,118	26.8	5,886	13.9	4,325	28.2
South Central (3)	10,417	18.8	7,105	37.1	8,508	20.1	5,018	32.7
North Central (2)	939	1.7	385	2.0	978	2.3	434	2.8
West (1)	7,869	14.2	1,820	9.5	6,276	14.8	1,636	10.7

Source: Table 3.

Note: Totals do not equal sum of entries due to the exclusion of all but 15 states.

Regional definitions: See Table 3.

The exact opposite can be observed in the South Central region between 1910 and 1970 where increases can be noted in both total and Negro employment within the region. These data illustrate the growing importance of both the New Orleans and Texas ports and the increasing number of Negro longshoremen in the area. A continuing upward trend could only mean more jobs for Negro longshoremen.

The West Coast presents an interesting case which illustrates the ability of a union to influence employment practices. The data shows that the total employment on West Coast docks has risen steadily since 1910, with the relative share of total employment increasing from 4.1 percent in 1910 to 14.8 percent in 1970. Negro employment, however, remained extremely low through 1940 and then increased tremendously thereafter. As will be detailed below, this can be attributed to the policy of the International Longshoremen's and Warehousemen's Union, formed in the late 1930's, and probably effectuated during World War II, after the census of 1940 was taken. Prior to the establishment of this policy, Negroes were rarely used on West Coast docks except in the role of strikebreakers. West Coast entries in Tables 3 and 4 include California employment data only because Negroes were not included in any other state of the region.

Indicative of the major role played by Negroes in the longshore industry is that the percent of black employment did not drop dramatically in any state, except Massachusetts, when total employment decreased and in some cases, the percent Negro increased as total employment decreased (see Tables 5 and 6). In New York, for example, between 1910 and 1920, when total employment increased by 102.4 percent, Negro employment increased by 385.2 percent. During the next decade, total employment decreased 41.1 percent and Negro employment decreased only 38.2 percent. Of course, there are negative connotations to this phenomenon, including the fact that only in difficult and casual labor markets could the Negro find acceptability, but it is important to note that in longshoring, the black man was not the first to go when cutbacks occurred.

Considerable caution must be exercised, however, in translating high levels of black employment into high levels of weekly or yearly earnings or weekly hours worked. Given that most ports were not decasualized through the mid-1950's, relatively few longshoremen achieved more than a subsistence earnings level.

TABLE 5. *Longshore Industry*
Total and Negro Employment for United States and Selected States,[a] *1910-1930*

State	1910			1920			1930		
	Total	Negro	Percent Negro	Total	Negro	Percent Negro	Total	Negro	Percent Negro
Total United States	62,813	16,379	26.1	85,605	27,206	31.8	73,944	25,434	34.4
Total Eight States	16,390	12,084	73.7	22,419	17,519	78.1	20,800	16,775[b]	80.6
Alabama	888	715	80.5	1,117	1,010	90.4	1,443	1,383	95.8
Florida	1,709	1,530	89.5	1,470	1,312	89.3	2,028	1,882	92.8
Georgia	1,762	1,683	95.5	1,799	1,680	93.4	1,608	1,554	96.6
Louisiana	2,654	1,588	59.8	4,390	2,862	65.2	5,322	3,953	74.3
Maryland	2,975	1,933	65.0	4,349	3,179	73.1	3,400	2,334	68.6
South Carolina	560	513	91.6	762	733	96.2	963	n.a.	—
Texas	2,386	843	35.3	3,601	2,052	57.0	3,926	2,739	69.8
Virginia	3,456	3,279	94.9	4,931	4,691	95.1	3,073	2,930	95.3
New York	18,545	1,119	6.0	37,526	5,429	14.5	22,119	3,357	15.2
New Jersey	4,984	136	2.7	4,977	383	7.7	4,477	542	12.1
Pennsylvania	3,522	1,428	40.5	4,224	2,409	57.0	4,345	2,252	51.8
Massachusetts	3,341	154	4.6	2,843	275	9.7	3,049	255	8.4
California	2,593	38	1.5	3,728	44	1.2	6,346	91	1.4

Source: *U.S. Census of Population:*

1910: Vol. IV, *Occupational Statistics,* Tables 6, 7.
1920: Vol. IV, *Occupations,* Table 1, pp. 875-1033, Table 6, p. 386, Table 10, p. 427.
1930: Vol. IV, *Occupations, by States,* Tables 4, 11, 13.

[a] Figures for employed males only.

[b] Seven states only; South Carolina data not available for Negroes, 963 total males excluded from total.

TABLE 6. *Longshore Industry*
Total and Negro Employment by Race for United States and Selected States,[a] *1940-1960*

State	1940 Total	1940 Negro	1940 Percent Negro	1950 Total	1950 Negro	1950 Percent Negro	1960 Total	1960 Negro	1960 Percent Negro
Total United States	63,241	20,279	32.1	62,003	21,197	34.2	55,479	19,129	34.5
Total Eight States	20,418	15,759	77.2	17,964	13,279	73.9	16,912	12,223	72.3
Alabama	1,272	1,173	92.2	1,112	1,036	93.2	1,080	1,027	95.1
Florida	2,845	2,645	93.0	1,658	1,434	86.5	1,543	1,272	82.4
Georgia	1,353	1,308	96.7	687	657	95.6	787	744	94.5
Louisiana	3,874	2,719	70.2	4,870	3,734	76.7	4,722	3,561	75.4
Maryland	3,358	2,016	60.0	3,445	2,314	67.2	2,117	1,248	59.0
South Carolina	748	729	97.5	504	479	95.0	607	583	96.0
Texas	4,393	2,790	63.5	4,044	2,142	53.0	4,615	2,517	54.5
Virginia	2,575	2,379	92.4	1,644	1,483	90.2	1,441	1,271	88.2
New York	16,242	1,509	9.3	18,105	2,643	14.6	13,638	2,014	14.8
New Jersey	3,816	463	12.1	3,839	509	13.3	3,524	421	11.9
Pennsylvania	3,273	1,342	41.0	3,152	1,502	47.7	2,156	1,120	51.9
Massachusetts	2,221	172	7.7	1,611	86	5.3	1,322	41	3.1
California	6,865	83	1.2	8,481	2,032	24.0	7,869	1,820	23.1

Source: *U.S. Census of Population*:

1940: Vol. III, *The Labor Force*, Part 1, U.S. Summary, Table 62; Part 2, Table 13, State Volumes, Parts 2-5, Table 13.
1950: Vol. II, *Characteristics of the Population*, Part 1, U.S. Summary, Table 128, State Volumes, Table 77.
1960: Vol. I, *Characteristics of the Population*, Part 1, U.S. Summary, Table 205, State Volumes, Table 122.

[a] Figures for employed males only.

Tables 7 and 8 present data for the 1970 census year and illustrates that the percent of black employment continued to increase over past figures. Table 7 illustrates that the percent of Negro employment decreased in most southern states but increased in New Jersey and California. These results are not surprising because during periods of declining employment (typical of longshoring between 1960 and 1970) it can be expected that Negroes would suffer greater job losses in areas where they comprise a large majority of the work force. The relative importance of New Jersey and California ports, however, increased over the period creating job opportunities for blacks.

BOSTON

More so than in any other major port, the Boston longshoremen have been dominated over the years by one ethnic group—the Irish. Maud Russell points out that many of the Irish immigrants "never went far from the docks on which they landed. [In 1966], so many years after the 'Great Migration,' the longshoremen of Boston retain an unmatched Irishness. . . ." [67]

According to Professor Northrup, there were unions of longshoremen in Boston as far back as 1847; however, by 1912, union rules were established that placed strict limits on union membership. He also noted that "Negroes and immigrants from southern or eastern Europe have never been welcomed into the old Irish-controlled locals." [68] Spero and Harris report that Negroes were used as strikebreakers against the Irish in Boston as far back as 1855.[69] E. D. Fite notes Negroes were used in Boston at an early stage.

> Negroes were also being displaced as stevedores and longshoremen because of the violent racial antipathy which was manifested by the Irish against the Negro workmen along the docks in such Northern cities as Cleveland, Detroit, Boston, New York, Brooklyn, Albany, and Chicago.[70]

---

67. Maud Russell, *Men Along the Shore* (New York: Brussel and Brussel, Inc., 1966), p. 244.

68. Herbert R. Northrup, *Organized Labor and the Negro* (New York: Kraus Reprint Co., 1971), p. 141.

69. Sterling D. Spero and Abram L. Harris, *The Black Worker* (New York: Atheneum, 1968), p. 148.

70. Lorenzo J. Greene and Carter G. Woodson, *The Negro Wage Earner* (1930; reprinted, New York: Russell and Russell, 1969), p. 23.

TABLE 7. *Longshore Industry*
Total and Negro Employment for United States and Selected States,[a] *1970*

State	Total	Negro	Percent Negro
Total United States	42,349	15,326	36.2
Total Eight States	14,394	9,343	64.9
Alabama	752	652	86.7
Florida	1,570	1,155	73.6
Georgia	672	564	83.9
Louisiana	3,644	2,499	68.6
Maryland	1,756	980	55.8
South Carol[illegible]	547	524	95.8
Texas	4,112	1,867	45.4
Virginia	1,341	1,102	82.2
New York	7,175	1,098	15.3
New Jersey	2,955	661	22.4
Pennsylvania	1,634	843	51.6
Massachusetts	766	4	0.5
California	6,276	1,636	26.1

Source: *U.S. Census of Population: 1970*, PC(1)-D, *Detailed Characteristics*, U.S. Summary, Table 223, State Volumes, Table 171.

[a] Figures for employed males only.

TABLE 8. *Longshore Industry*
Percent Distribution of Total and Negro Employment[a] *by Region Selected States, 1970*

Region	Total	Percent	Negro	Percent
Total United States	42,349	100.0	15,326	100.0
Northeast (4)	12,530	29.6	2,606	17.0
South Atlantic (5)	5,886	13.9	4,325	28.2
South Central (3)	8,508	20.1	5,018	32.7
North Central (2)	978	2.3	434	2.8
West (1)	6,276	14.8	1,636	10.7

Source: *U.S. Census of Population: 1970*, PC(1)-D, *Detailed Characteristics*, U.S. Summary, Table 223, State Volumes, Table 171.

Regional definitions: See Table 3, p. 35.

[a] Figures for employed males only.

Apparently, Negroes had made some gains on the Boston waterfront that the Irish were attempting to reduce. In fact, the Negro presence on the Boston waterfront extends as far back as 1830. Greene and Woodson report that there were two Negro stevedores in the city during that census year.[71] It is interesting to note that the Irish have been extremely successful in maintaining their superiority on the Boston docks in the face of challenges not only by Negroes but also by Italians. In other New England areas, such as New Bedford, Massachusetts, the Italians were dominant and the Poles were also strong in longshore work.[72]

The first longshore union in the country was established in Boston in 1847 as the Boston Longshoremen's Provident Union.[73] Although it began as a benevolent organization, it soon became a regular labor union and in 1882 engaged in a partially successful strike.[74] In 1886, the Knights of Labor organized three assemblies of Boston waterfront employees and in 1912, these three assemblies and the Provident Union affiliated with the International Longshoremen's Association.[75]

It is highly doubtful that Negroes played an important role in these unions or that they were even organized. According to Russell, ". . . the almost all-Irish Longshoremen's Provident Union waged such an unrelenting battle against the immigrants that it succeeded in keeping Latin workmen off the docks for generations." [76] It seems reasonable to conclude that if the Irish were protective of their jobs against Italians, they would also be protective against Negro longshoremen. This is corroborated by Barnes who notes that

As the unions will not admit Italians or Negroes to membership, it follows that there are practically none of these people employed in foreign commerce work. The coastwise men, much less important as a class, are

71. *Ibid.*, Table 1, p. 5.

72. Russell, *op. cit.*, p. 244.

73. Charles B. Barnes, *The Longshoremen* (New York: The Russell Sage Foundation, 1915), pp. 183-184.

74. *Ibid.*, p. 184.

75. *Ibid.*

76. Russell, *op. cit.*, p. 47.

unorganized and of a somewhat different racial composition. Among them are Portuguese, Pol[es], Italians, Negroes, and a few Irish.[77]

It probably was the Negro coastwise longshoremen that Daniels was referring to when he noted that in 1900:

> The members of [the Laborers] subdivision who earn the most are the longshoremen, who load and unload cargoes of all sorts along the water front. Some of them do not have assured steady work, but are taken on intermittently at certain docks where no regular force is kept, or elsewhere as extra hands. . . . Thus many of them manage to bring their weekly earnings up to $15 or $20.[78]

The number of men referred to, however, must have been small since the subdivision "laborers not attached to any particular industry" contained only 665 entries and the 1910 census listed only 154 Negro longshoremen in the state of Massachusetts. Daniels does point out that unionism did not escape all Negro dockworkers in Boston around the turn of the century.

> There used to be a union among the meat-loaders about the docks which included both Negroes and whites, but it was disrupted as a result of attempting strike tactics. At present there are several longshoremen's unions which have Negro members, but for the same reason of the excess of supply of such labor, these amount to little.[79]

The work in Boston, as in most other ports, has always been separated into foreign commerce—deep sea foreign trade—and coastwise trade. In 1915, Barnes observed that most of the deep sea work was performed by the Irish and that their union strongly controlled entrance to the trade.[80] It is interesting to note that the coastwise trade was not completely organized until after 1935 and that in 1941, 12 percent of total ILA membership in Massachusetts were Negro, the highest percentage of any union organized in Massachusetts.[81] It is probably that the increase in Negro participation in the ILA stems from their use as strikebreakers in 1929.

---

77. Barnes, *op. cit.*, p. 181.

78. John Daniels, *In Freedom's Birthplace*, reprinted in The American Negro: His History and Literature series (New York: Arno Press and the New York Times, 1969), pp. 335-336.

79. *Ibid.*, p. 378.

80. Barnes, *op. cit.*, p. 181.

81. Northrup, *op. cit.*, pp. 141-142.

During August 1929 the white longshoremen of Boston struck, when asked to double their loads. 125 Negroes were hired to replace the strikers. Because no Negroes ever had a "real chance" to work on the Boston docks, this was regarded as an opportunity to secure such employment as well as union protection.[82]

The census data presented earlier conflict somewhat with the above findings. The black percentage of total longshore employment in Massachusetts was 8.4 percent in 1930 and 7.7 percent in 1940. (See Tables 5 and 6.) In Boston for the same years, black participation rates were 8.6 percent and 8.7 percent respectively.[83] Given that Negroes were concentrated in the coastwise trade that remained outside of union organization, the 12 percent figure for Negro participation in the ILA may be overstated.

The port of Boston has never exploited its natural competitive advantage over other East Coast ports. Boston is the closest American port to Europe and its natural harbor offers easy access to its docks. The distance between open water and dockside is shortest in Boston compared to other East Coast ports. Partially responsible for the declining position of Boston's waterfront has been the union's successful fight against mechanization. The fear of job reductions led the ILA to oppose cargo handling innovation to the extent that through the 1960's, Boston was the only major port in the country handling cargo with pre-1930 techniques.[84] Prior to 1968, Boston longshoremen refused to handle palletized break-bulk cargo, resulting in the inefficient use of forklift trucks and the wasting of vital gang manpower.[85] The end result was higher labor costs, slower ship turnaround time, and a declining volume of waterfront business. Symptomatic of the union's desire to impede technological advancement is that a jurisdictional dispute between the ILA and the Teamsters Union caused a modern container terminal, built by Sea-

82. Ira DeA. Reid, *Negro Membership in American Labor Unions* (New York: National Urban League, 1930), p. 168.

83. *U. S. Census of Population: 1930,* Vol. IV., *Occupations, by States,* Table 12; *1940,* Vol. III, *The Labor Force,* Part 1, Tables 11, 13, 58, 62.

84. U. S. Department of Labor, *Manpower Utilization—Job Security in the Longshore Industry, Boston* (Washington: 1964), pp. 42-43.

85. Lewis M. Schneider, "The Port of Boston in the 1970's," mimeographed case study, Harvard Business School, 1970, p. 3.

Land in 1966, to remain completely idle.[86] As of 1970 this facility still had not received its first ship,[87] but since then it has been working regularly.

Ironically, the desire to protect jobs actually contributed to reductions in work opportunities for Boston longshoremen as more and more cargo was shifted to the Port of New York and to other areas. The census data reveal that there has been a steady, major decrease in longshore employment in the state of Massachusetts over the past forty years. (See Table 9.) In conjunction with decasualization, occurring during the mid-1960's, the effect of ILA job protection activities has been catastrophic in terms of Negro employment. The data in Tables 5 through 7 reveal that although total employment on the Massachusetts waterfront decreased by 77.1 percent between 1910 and 1970, Negro employment virtually disappeared during the same period. It is important to note that decasualization is primarily responsible for the decrease occurring between 1960 and 1970 only, and that the decline of work opportunities in the port of Boston began at least 30 years before decasualization was attempted. ILA control of work rules and practices contributed heavily to the decline. In terms of the decline of Negro employment in Boston longshoring, it is quite possible that the increase of firms utilizing unskilled and semiskilled labor in and around Boston in the 1950's in addition to the firm entrenchment of the Irish on the Boston waterfront eliminated many Negro longshore jobs. It is interesting to note Maud Russell's claim that many Negroes have operated under the ILA banner since 1964. "The newest ILA branch, #1908, chartered in 1964, is headed by George Hall and Edward F. Lesniak and its many Negro members represent yet another minority group that has made major contributions to American shipping." [88] It is apparent that the Negro members of this local did not survive very long in longshorework, or else escaped census tabulation, since the 1970 census revealed only four black longshoremen in the state of Massachusetts!

The only available Equal Employment Opportunity Commission data confirm the fact that Negroes have virtually disappeared from the Massachusetts waterfront. (See Table 10.) Although these data probably do not represent the entire Massachusetts longshore

86. Lewis M. Schneider, *The Problem of the Port of Boston* (Cambridge: Harvard Business School, 1968), pp. 44-48).

87. Schneider, "The Port of Boston in the 1970's," *op. cit.*, p. 4.

88. Russell, *op. cit.*, p. 244.

TABLE 9. *Longshore Industry*
Total and Negro Employment
Massachusetts, 1910-1970

	1910	1920	1930	1940	1950	1960	1970
Total	3,341	2,843	3,049	2,221	1,611	1,322	766
Negro	154	275	255	172	86	41	4
Percent Negro	4.6	9.7	8.4	7.7	5.3	3.1	0.5

Source: Tables 5, 6, 7, pp. 41, 42, 44.

TABLE 10. *Longshore Industry*
Employment by Race and Occupational Group
Massachusetts, 1966 and 1969 [a]

Occupational Group	1966 Total [b]	1966 Negro	1966 Percent Negro	1969 Total	1969 Negro	1969 Percent Negro
Officials and managers	19	1	5.3	18	—	—
Professionals	2	—	—	3	—	—
Technicians	—	—	—	—	—	—
Sales workers	—	—	—	—	—	—
Office and clerical	39	—	—	17	—	—
Total white collar	60	1	1.7	38	—	—
Craftsmen	55	—	—	28	—	—
Operatives	13	5	38.5	4	—	—
Laborers	1,008	51	5.1	1,672	—	—
Service workers	—	—	—	—	—	—
Total blue collar	1,076	56	5.2	1,704	—	—
Total	1,136	57	5.0	1,742	—	—

Source: U.S. Equal Employment Opportunity Commission, 1966, 1969.

[a] These data cover 4 establishments in 1966 and 5 establishments in 1969.

[b] Includes males and females, although the number of females in the industry is very small.

work force, the sample size is sufficiently large to be, together with the census data, reasonable proof of the decline of blacks on the Massachusetts waterfront. The increasing sample size from 1966 to 1969 should not be construed as increasing employment opportunities, since the sample sizes were different for each year.

It is clear that although blacks have had a history of employment in Massachusetts longshoring, several forces operate to have reduced black employment close to extinction. The most important features include the dominance of the Irish on the docks, strict control of the labor supply by the union through limited membership procedures, strong union resistance to mechanization, and the effects of decasualization. The first two features operated to limit the number of Negroes who could find employment under any economic conditions and the second two features acted to reduce the number of job opportunities available to anyone of any race.

NEW YORK

The Port of New York is the largest port in the country in terms of both land area and number of waterfront employees. For much of the history of waterborne transportation in this country, New York received and dispatched the major portion. In recent years, the Manhattan area of the Port of New York has declined in importance as passenger ships disappeared and as larger cargo ships and the advent of containerization forced ship operators to look elsewhere for bigger and more modern dock facilities. As was noted earlier, this changing technology had a positive effect, rather than the usual negative effect, upon the importance of the black longshoreman to the industry.

Early New York Longshoremen

According to George E. Haynes, both indentured and free Negroes were employed on the docks in the New Amsterdam Colony in 1628 and aboard vessels of the Dutch West India Company.[89] This early introduction to the longshore industry formed the foundation of a black history on the New York waterfront, but historians disagree over its relative importance. According to Albon Man, 1840-1950's saw New York longshore occupations solely in the hands of blacks.[90] He also reported that black-white anamocities during the 1850's became pronounced because of the role Negroes played as strikebreakers. However, once the employers achieved their purpose, the Negroes were discharged from these new jobs and only a few remain to work on the docks.[91] If, indeed, the New York longshore industry was dominated by blacks in the 1840's and 1850's, the loss of control and the reduction in status to that of strikebreaker must have occurred almost overnight.

The strike Man mentions was not the first to occur in New York City nor was the organization involved.

The earliest longshore strike of which there is historical record took place in 1836. "In 1836 the longshoremen, riggers, and other employees con-

---

89. George P. Haynes, *The Negro at Work in New York City*, reprinted in The American Negro: His History and Literature series (New York: Arno Press and the New York Times, 1968), p. 66.

90. Albon P. Man, Jr., "Labor Competition and the New York Draft Riots of 1863," *Journal of Negro History*, Vol. XXXVI (October 1851), p. 376.

91. *Ibid.*, p. 394.

nected with shipping in New York, struck for an increase of wages and less hours, and upon finding that their places were being taken by others *not members of their organizations,* they went from wharf to wharf, first requesting the workmen to leave their work, and then it is claimed threatened them. . . . The men were finally obliged to return to work under much the same conditions as when they struck." [92]

It is highly improbable that Negro longshoremen were not included in these organizations; and if they were on the waterfront, they probably were among the strikebreakers. Most authorities agree that the introduction of Negroes to the New York waterfront was through their use as strikebreakers after the 1840's.[93] Spero and Harris pointed out that the Negro presence on the waterfront served to arouse the resentment of the white longshoremen to such a degree that violence and bloodshed resulted.[94] As noted earlier, however, these Negro longshore jobs were temporary since most of the strikers returned to their jobs when the stoppage ended.

The most predominant white longshore group on the New York waterfront at this time was the Irish. They were generally employed at low-skill jobs and, therefore, resented the competition which they feared from blacks.[95] Any successful inroads made by the Negro would have served to reduce further the already scarce job opportunities available to the Irish. Because of this, it was probably the Irish who in March 1853 filed a certificate of incorporation as the "Alongshoremen's United Benefit Society." [96] According to Russell, "Its greatest success seems to have been in the filling out of its legal forms, for nothing else is ever heard of it." [97]

The fear of potential Negro dominance over the New York waterfront played a role in the 1860 election campaign. In an

---

92. Barnes, *op. cit.*, p. 93, emphasis added, quoting George E. McNeill, *The Labor Movement* (Boston: A.M. Bridgeman and Co., 1887), pp. 87-88.

93. See, for example, Spero and Harris, *op. cit.*, p. 197; Northrup, *op. cit.*, p. 142; and Charles H. Wesley, *Negro Labor in the United States, 1850-1925* (New York: Vanguard Press, 1927), pp. 79-80. Wesley, however, notes that black longshoremen, among others, were members of the New York African Society for Mutual Relief, founded in 1808 and chartered in 1810. *Ibid.*, p. 203.

94. Spero and Harris, *op. cit.*, p. 197.

95. *Ibid.*, pp. 197-198.

96. Russell, *op. cit.*, p. 17.

97. *Ibid.*

effort to insure the defeat of Republican candidates, southern spokesmen were brought to New York to appeal to the fears of the Irish. They claimed that slaves would soon be found in all types of labor and would begin to compete for jobs held by white people now employed.[98]

The appeal was ineffective, but it is not known whether the expected influx of Negroes to the waterfront actually occurred. What is known, however, is that in 1863 another longshore strike was broken by the use of Negro strikebreakers.[99] These strikebreakers were most probably emancipated slaves imported from the south.[100]

In 1864, the Irish waterfront workers formed the Alongshoremen's Union Protective Association which later became known as LUPA after dropping the "a" from alongshoremen. LUPA continued in existence through 1886 as a loosely structured organization composed of autonomous locals located throughout the Port of New York. The unsuccessful strike in 1874 seriously weakened its effectiveness and total membership.[101] According to Russell, LUPA created a separate division, Branch 6, for "colored only."[102]

In 1885, the Knights of Labor began to organize New York longshoremen, achieving their greatest success among the coastwise longshoremen.[103] The regular longshoremen, *i.e.* those engaged in foreign commerce, quickly followed suit and for some time, many longshoremen belonged to both LUPA and the Knights of Labor. It is possible that Negroes working in the coastwise trade were organized. An ill-fated strike in 1887, however, doomed unionism almost entirely for the next ten years.

One facet of the 1887 strike was the boycotting of Old Dominion Steamship Line as a reaction to a change in wage payment from hourly to weekly. In a law suit, the company charged that ". . . the boycott was maintained for the purpose of procuring the same wages for Negro workers in southern ports that longshoremen

---

98. Man, *op. cit.*, p. 378.

99. Spero and Harris, *op. cit.*, p. 198.

100. Man, *op. cit.*, p. 386.

101. Barnes, *op. cit.*, p. 99.

102. Russell, *op. cit.*, p. 108.

103. Barnes, *op. cit.*, p. 101.

earned in New York."[104] Old Dominion maintained operations in New York and Newport News, Virginia. Interestingly, Old Dominion imported blacks from southern ports to serve as strikebreakers in New York which led to another flare-up of racial hatred.[105]

It was during the port-wide strike of 1887 that the Irish dominance of the waterfront began to diminish. It was then that the shipping companies

> . . . turned to Italians to break the "big strike," led by the Knights of Labor. Several lines also used Negro strike breakers on this occasion. . . . Six years later, in an extensive strike in Brooklyn, Italians and Negroes brought from the South were again used as strike breakers, but it was the former, who had been becoming an increasingly important factor in the industry for the past six years, who really broke the strike.[106]

So great was the Italian influx that by the end of 1887, Italians comprised fully one-third of the total New York waterfront employment.[107] Although Negroes had been present on the New York waterfront for many years prior to this, it was the Italian, and not the Negro, who broke the Irish dominance of the trade. Negroes had still not gained a permanent foothold in New York longshore employment. It is interesting to note, however, that the Irish reacted to the Italians in much the same fashion as they reacted to the Negro. According to Barnes:

> Separated as it was, by race and language, from sympathy with the older workers, a gang of Italians was found to have a deterrent effect [upon the Irish]. The Irish were afraid of Italian competition. The fear lessened the likelihood of a strike and kept the men from actively resenting abuses.[108]

Although the likelihood of a port-wide organized strike may have been lessened by the introduction of Italians, Russell explains that many small and short-lived walkouts occurred with Irish men refusing to work with Italian gangs or simply walking off the piers when it was rumored that Italians were to be hired.[109] Spero and

104. Russell, *op. cit.*, p. 35.

105. *Ibid.*, p. 38.

106. Spero and Harris, *op. cit.*, pp. 198-199.

107. Barnes, *op. cit.*, p. 5.

108. *Ibid.*, p. 6.

109. Russell, *op. cit.*, pp. 46-47.

Harris also report that much violence occurred in 1887 between Irish strikers and Italian strikebreakers.[110]

There were sporadic attempts made to organize the Port of New York subsequent to the demise of the Knights of Labor, but none were successful until the ILA appeared around the turn of the century. It is this union that brought permanent organization to the New York waterfront.

1900 to World War II

The role of the Negro on the New York waterfront prior to 1900 was confined to that of strikebreaker with little permanent attachment accruing to Negroes as a result. Their use in a similar capacity in 1895, however, resulted in permanent gains since the Ward Line continued to employ Negroes long after the strike had ended.[111] Subsequent strikes in 1899 and 1907 resulted in further permanent gains. The increased use of Negro longshoremen may have been quite rapid and one observer noted that [t]here are thousands of Negroes on the docks of New York." [112]

Union organization increased rapidly as the newly formed ILA began to absorb the remaining LUPA locals composed almost entirely of Italians; in 1914, the LUPA and the ILA finally merged. According to Russell:

> The ILA did not fall into the error of offending or neglecting minority groups. Aware of the closeness of Italian workers, ILA organizers formed locals in Brooklyn which were 99 per cent Italian. Negroes, still almost exclusively engaged in coastwise work, were not placed in separate divisions, as LUPA had done in forming its Branch 6 for "colored only." [113]

Whether many Negroes were organized at all at the time of the merger is open to question, since the coastwise segment of the longshore industry did not come under ILA jurisdiction until 1916. According to another authority:

> In the Port of New York, concessions were made to the ethnically oriented locals while seeking to avoid their former divisiveness. With

110. Spero and Harris, *op. cit.*, p. 199.

111. Northrup, *op. cit.*, p. 142.

112. Mary White Ovington, *Half a Man: The Status of the Negro in New York City* (1911; reprint ed. New York: Schocken Books, 1969), p. 85.

113. Russell, *op. cit.*, p. 108.

ILA affiliations, the "white" longshoremen, Irish, Scandinavian, and German, were reported performing hold and deck work, while the foreign born Italians were performing the less skilled dock work, increasingly hold work, but virtually no deck work. Negroes were employed in the most unskilled tasks of trucking on the docks, or in *unorganized coastwise trades.*[114]

Partially in response to the desire of the ILA to remove the threat of Negro strikebreakers and partially because many blacks were working in the coastwise trades that were being newly organized, the Negro became an important part of the ILA in New York. Also responsible for the growth in importance of the Negro longshoreman was the labor shortage created by World War I. Discrimination, however, continued to exist in the form of the "expressed preference" for white longshoremen on the part of some shippers in the port.[115]

As late as 1930, Spero and Harris reported that

> There are many piers in New York which refuse to employ Negroes. Most piers which do employ Negroes work four or five Negro gangs along with eighteen or twenty white gangs. . . . Some companies have tried to use black labor as a club against their white workers. . . . Stevedores, like many employers, frequently become accustomed to employing labor belonging to particular racial groups. Thus the Kerr Line in New York employ only Italians. Other lines prefer Irish or Hungarians or Slovaks, and will take workers from these groups if they are available. Frequently, when Negroes unable to get work on certain piers lay the fact to race prejudice they are really suffering from such prejudice no more than groups of white workers who do not happen to belong to the nationality to which the stevedore has become accustomed.[116]

The shape-up and the system of choosing laborers through gang foremen aggrevated the problem.

The influx of Negro longshoremen and the concomitant increase in the importance of the new workers, however, are undeniable. As can be seen in Table 11, the participation rate of Negro longshoremen increased quite dramatically between 1910 and 1920.[117] The wartime manpower shortage was obviously responsi-

---

114. Joseph P. Goldberg, "Modernization in the Maritime Industry," in Harold M. Levenson *et al., Collective Bargaining and Technological Change in American Transportation* (Evanston, Ill.: The Transportation Center, Northwestern University, 1971), p. 278, emphases added.

115. Northrup, *op. cit.*, p. 143.

116. Spero and Harris, *op. cit.*, p. 200.

117. These census data do not represent the universe of longshore employment in New York. The census undercount is unexplainable, but none-

ble for this increase because as whites found jobs in other industries, blacks migrated North in search of the vacant positions.

Union organization along ethnic lines continued through the end of World War I and the 1920's. The stronghold of Negro union organization was Local 968 in Brooklyn, claiming some 1,000 Negro members during this period.[118] Of course, Negroes were located in other sections of the port, but the largest single body was found in Local 968. One source estimated the port-wide Negro strength in 1926 at approximately 6,000 workers.[119] In relation to the dispersion of Negro longshoremen throughout the port, MacElwee and Taylor note that "Negroes are ordinarily placed in groups by themselves, but it is not uncommon to see them in holds working with Germans, Greeks, . . . and others." [120]

Interestingly, the desire to prevent Negroes from acting as strikebreakers that led ultimately to their organization did not free the union from such occurrences. An unauthorized strike in the late 1920's saw more than 500 black strikebreakers employed on piers that generally employed Irish workers. The strikebreakers received more in hourly wages than the strikers, but they were not retained on these piers once the strike ended.[121] This fact, coupled with the recognized admission of Negroes to the union as a means of survival, indicates that blacks were tolerated in the port rather than accepted on an equal basis. It is important to recognize, however, that union membership and local division along racial and ethnic lines allowed for the development of influential and powerful black union officials. According to Spero and Harris:

> The leaders of the Negro longshoremen in New York . . . prefer to have the members of their race join their own locals because it gives them direct representation and power and influence in both district and international councils which they would not have if they remained minorities scattered in various white unions.[122]

---

theless exists for the entire 1910-1970 period. The participation rates and trends, however, are probably accurate.

118. Reid, *op. cit.*, p. 49.

119. Greene and Woodson, *op. cit.*, p. 308. These data were collected by the authors and are not comparable with census data.

120. Roy S. MacElwee and Thomas R. Taylor, *Wharf Management—Stevedoring and Storage* (New York: D. Appleton and Co., 1921), p. 56.

121. Reid, *op. cit.*, p. 168.

122. Spero and Harris, *op. cit.*, p. 202.

TABLE 11. *Longshore Industry*
Total and Negro Employment
New York, 1910-1970

	1910	1920	1930	1940	1950	1960	1970
Total	18,545	37,526	22,119	16,242	18,105	13,638	7,175
Negro	1,119	5,429	3,357	1,509	2,643	2,014	1,098
Percent Negro	6.0	14.5	15.2	9.3	14.6	14.8	15.3

Source: Tables, 5, 6, 7, pp. 41, 42, 44.

The Negro locals were actually an extension of the ethnic divisions developed earlier by LUPA.[123]

The ILA in 1935 reported that Negroes comprised 12.4 percent of Manhattan's total longshore labor force.[124] Of the seven ILA locals registered, Negroes became a major force in only two: Local 791, general longshore; and Local 1258, coastwise longshore.[125] Local 791 was organized in 1902 and admitted its first Negro in 1925; however, prior to 1925, Negroes were affiliated with the separate Local 875.[126] According to Charles L. Franklin, Negroes were allowed membership in Local 791 in order to prevent employers from using them as strikebreakers. On the other hand, Local 1258, which was organized in 1934, has always admitted Negroes.[127]

As already noted, many Negro longshoremen were organized into Brooklyn Local 968, which was chartered by the ILA in 1915, and listed several black officers and officials as members. There is some doubt about the relative importance of the black longshoremen in Local 968. Census data for 1920 and 1930 reveal Negro participation rates in Brooklyn of 8.2 percent and 6.4 percent respectively; however, on a port-wide bases, these rates were 14.5 percent and 15.2 percent which is somewhat higher in both cases.[128] Although there may possibly be an error in the census data, the wide disparity between Brooklyn and the entire New York port area indicates that Negroes participated in the industry to a greater extent in areas other than Brooklyn.

World War II to 1970

The 1930-1940 period witnessed a decline in New York longshore employment and with it a decline in the relative position of the black longshoreman. The onset of World War II and the

---

123. *Ibid.*, p. 203.

124. Charles L. Franklin, *The Negro Labor Unionist in New York* (New York: Columbia University Press, 1936), Table 16, p. 165.

125. *Ibid.*

126. *Ibid.*, pp. 189-190.

127. *Ibid.*, and p. 327.

128. *U. S. Census of Population: 1920*, Vol. IV, *Occupations*, Chapter VII, Tables 1, 2; *1930*, Vol. IV, *Occupations by States*, Tables 4, 11, 12.

resulting manpower shortage renewed the trend experienced during World War I. According to an industry spokesman, most Negroes gained permanent entrance to the New York waterfront during World War II and not earlier, as was previously presented.[129] The data in Table 11, covering the 1940-1950 period, confirmed the fact that the relative position of black longshoremen did improve. The strength of the ILA improved also during World War II.

The shape-up remained as the basic hiring mechanism, causing continued employment irregularity and hidden practices of discrimination. According to Larrowe:

> Under the shape-up, it was virtually impossible to prove charges of discrimination, but some evidence indicates that it was practiced. During World War II, ILA officials organized a Jim Crow local (824-1) for Negro longshoremen to whom Local 824 refused membership. Local 968, largely composed of Negro members, in addition to (unsuccessfully) filing charges of discrimination with the New York State Commission Against Discrimination, pointed to the fact that it was the only ILA local in the port which did not have exclusive jurisdiction over a pier.[130]

Local 968 was subsequently merged with Brooklyn Local 1814, on the promise that blacks in the local would be given their own pier. By 1960, these Negroes had still not received that pier.[131]

Documentation of the difficulty faced by Local 968 prior to its merger is contained in the testimony given to the Board of Inquiry established by the State of New York in 1952.

> The present longshore work force is composed of all types of workers in terms of age, national origin and race. . . . Several locals of the International Longshoremen's Association are composed predominantly of Italian-Americans and a few are predominantly Negro. One of the Negro locals, No. 968, in Brooklyn has recently been involved with other locals in a dispute over the fact that the membership has had trouble getting work.[132]

One researcher attributes the cause of the difficulty to the method of job distribution, *i.e.* the shape-up and gang structure, wherein

---

129. Interview, September 19, 1973.

130. Charles P. Larrowe, *Shape-up and Hiring Hall* (Berkeley: University of California Press, 1955), p. 72.

131. Herman D. Bloch, *The Circle of Discrimination* (New York: New York University Press, 1969), p. 118.

132. Board of Inquiry on Longshore Industry Work Stoppage October-November 1951, Port of New York, "Final Report to the Industrial Commissioner," State of New York, January 22, 1952, p. 56.

the hiring boss was free to develop his own choice criteria which frequently involved racial and ethnic prejudices.[133] The fact that Local 968 merged is illustrative not only of the problems of a black local, but also of the manner in which Negro locals were wooed by ILA officials interested in a higher union office. Thus, Professor Jensen comments about the maneuverings of Anthony Anastasia, late head of Brooklyn Local 1814:

> Anastasia had still other notions. He set out to woo the Negroes, not just in Brooklyn but in the South, as well. To do so he had to overcome a clash he had had with Clifford Robinson, president of all-Negro Local 968, who had denounced him when he refused to give the local a pier of its own. Anastasia had had to deny the request, for it was impossible to take a pier away from men who held it. Anastasia had simply said that to grant the request would "further perpetuate segregation" and "lead to unfortunate results." But Robinson had curtly rejoined, "Your remarks about segregating Negroes reveal a hypocrisy equaled only by your own dedication to keeping the Negro in a position apart." Anastasia later invited the Negro local to merge with Local 1814, and Robinson and the other officers agreed. When asked why, Robinson simply said, "Anastasia is the big man in Brooklyn and we don't get any support from the International." Anastasia, of course, gave some jobs to leaders from the Negro local.[134]

Anastasia failed, nevertheless, to gain black support in his attempt to win the ILA presidency. Since then, at each convention, aspiring ILA office seekers have taken positions in order to gain official support of black locals, and George Dixon, Negro head of the Mobile local, has attempted without success, to win one of the two top ILA offices which continue in the hands of white New York incumbents.[135]

In 1953, an agreement between the states of New York and New Jersey led to the formation of the Port of New York Waterfront Commission. The primary objectives of this new agency were to decasualize employment on the waterfront and to regularize the earnings and hours of those remaining attached to the industry. The methods adopted by the agency included a seniority system which protected those who worked regularly on one pier, and

---

133. Robert Lampson, "The 1951 New York Wildcat Dock Strike: Some Consequences of Union Structure for Management Labor Relations," *The Southwestern Social Science Quarterly*, Vol. XXXIV (March 1954), p. 35.

134. Vernon N. Jensen, *Strife on the Waterfront* (Ithaca, New York: Cornell University Press, 1974), p. 232.

135. *Ibid.*, pp. 288-289, 338.

establishment of hiring halls and a register that listed all the longshoremen working in the port. This register contained the names of all men who worked a minimum of 700 hours the previous year; those who did not meet this requirement were dropped, thus, achieving the first phase of decasualization.

Although the effects of decasualization on employment in the New York longshore industry have been numerous, it is not entirely responsible for the employment changes occuring within the industry. According to data published by the Board of Inquiry, total employment reported by the firms of the New York Shipping Association tapered off after World War II, decreasing from 71,476 in 1945-1946 to 41,995 in 1949-1950.[136] In 1955, during the first phase of decasualization, more than 50,000 men were attached to the New York waterfront, but by 1971, approximately 17,500 men remained.[137] Census data in Table 11, although not comparable to the Board's figures, corroborate the downward trend in employment which commenced prior to the establishment of a decasualization plan.

Longshoremen and checkers have also experienced a marked increase in average yearly earnings. Exclusive of fringe benefits, yearly earnings increased from $5,174 during 1960-1961 to $10,196 during 1970-1971, and the hourly wage rates increased from $3.00 per hour to $4.45 per hour during the same periods.[138] However, by 1973, the rate had increased to a record high of $5.55 per hour.

It is important to note that as total employment decreased, black participation remained relatively stable during the twenty-year period. The available data indicate that the effects of decasualization and declining employment extended to all components of the work force, and that Negroes were not disproportionately affected. Equal Employment Opportunity Commission data, on the other hand, indicate a level of Negro employment below that found in the census data (see Table 12). The EEOC data, however, covered a very small number of firms in the New York City standard metropolitan statistical area (SMSA), therefore, should not be considered representative of the entire industry. These data point out the fact that Negroes have made very little gains in white

136. Board of Inquiry, *op. cit.*, Table 2, p. 51.

137. Waterfront Commission of New York Harbor, *1971-72 Annual Report* (New York: 1972), pp. 16-19.

138. *Ibid.*, p. 16.

TABLE 12. *Longshore Industry*
Employment by Race and Occupational Group
New York City SMSA, 1964, 1966, 1969, 1970 [a]

Occupational Group	1964			1966			1969			1970		
	Total [b]	Negro	Percent Negro	Total [b]	Negro	Percent Negro	Total [b]	Negro	Percent Negro	Total [b]	Negro	Percent Negro
Officials and managers	29	—	—	74	—	—	257	—	—	353	1	0.3
Professionals	8	—	—	3	—	—	410	1	0.2	612	23	3.8
Technicians	3	—	—	—	—	—	51	4	7.8	136	6	4.4
Sales workers	—	—	—	5	—	—	31	—	—	47	—	—
Office and clerical	106	1	0.9	191	1	0.5	924	38	4.1	837	58	6.9
Total white collar	146	1	0.7	273	1	0.4	1,673	43	2.6	1,985	88	4.4
Craftsmen	—	—	—	—	—	—	95	3	3.2	542	84	15.5
Operatives	671	6	0.9	1,820	10	0.5	508	22	4.3	1,047	156	14.9
Laborers	949	167	17.6	7,445	575	7.7	341	36	10.6	570	132	23.2
Service workers	250	20	8.0	9	8	88.9	171	57	33.3	155	74	47.7
Total blue collar	1,870	193	10.3	9,274	593	6.4	1,115	118	10.6	2,314	446	19.3
Total	2,016	194	9.6	9,547	594	6.2	2,788	161	5.8	4,299	534	12.4

Source: U.S. Equal Employment Opportunity Commission, 1964, 1966, 1969, 1970.

[a] These data cover 7 establishments in 1964, 9 establishments in 1966, 22 establishments in 1969, and 20 establishments in 1970.

[b] Includes males and females, although the number of females in the industry is small.

collar employment in firms performing stevedore work. The laborer category, in which most longshoremen appear, showed a consistently high level of black participation.

Effects of Technology and Declining Employment

As noted in Chapter II, containerization has been the most influential technological advance made in the longshore industry. Containerization reduced substantially the number of men needed to load or unload a particular ship. If experiences with technological advancement in other industries were used as guides to predict the effects of containerization on Negroes in New York longshoring, it would be expected that many Negroes would be separated from the industry. In fact, however, containerization, along with other factors, has operated to expand job opportunities for Negroes in the Port of New York.

Container facilities require greater land areas for operation than conventional longshoring methods. Since the necessary land was generally unavailable for container terminal construction in Manhattan, ship operators and government agencies turned to the New Jersey side of the port in order to develop container facilities. Because the longshore industry in New Jersey, especially the ports of Newark and Elizabeth, had a higher representation of blacks than on the New York side, the result was an expansion of job opportunities for Negroes as more and more cargo was diverted to these facilities from the New York side of the harbor. The data in Table 13 confirm this heavy concentration of Negroes in New Jersey longshoring.

Containerization is not the only factor aiding black employment on the New Jersey side of the port. According to Professor Jensen:

> . . . Port Newark is . . . unique since it does not have the customary finger piers. It is a developed port area with continuous wharves or a succession of berths. . . .Because a rotation system of hiring had been forced upon them a number of years earlier, gangs had not laid claim to rights at certain berths. . . . When the [Waterfront] commission began its operations in December 1953, the ILA had controlled two local unions, one of which was a "white" local and the other a Negro local. Each local carried fifteen gangs; and, roughly speaking, the work was divided between them. Work was assigned on the basis of rotation in each local, this practice having been instituted about 1940, in a high-handed way by the union business agent.[139]

139. Vernon H. Jensen, *Hiring of Dock Workers and Employment Practices in the Ports of New York, Liverpool, London, Rotterdam and*

After the attempted take over of the New York locals by the AFL-CIO sponsored union, this system changed and employers listed with the waterfront commission the gangs they considered "theirs," and gave preference in hiring them.[140]

At the present time in the Port Newark area, there are two key locals: Local 1235, "white," which is composed of some men of Italian descent, but is becoming more a Puerto Rican or Spanish-surnamed local; and Local 1233, an all-black local. These two locals perform work for Sea-Land, the area's largest employer. Because individual piers did not exist in Port Newark, the earlier arriving whites were unable to establish "ownership" of a territory or pier, as they did in New York City. Moreover, the seniority system developed along with the decasualization plan, which inhibits the movement of longshoremen throughout the port, operated further to increase these job opportunities. Longshoremen from the New York side who moved to the New Jersey side in order to seek longshore jobs, were not entitled to work until all regular gangs for that area found employment.

As of November 1973, black Local 1233 at Port Newark, had 970 members, and white Local 1235, listed 1,400 members with the work division system still enforced. Thus, it would appear that there is reverse discrimination in the setup, the opposite of what we shall find was traditional in other ports such as Baltimore, New Orleans, and Galveston. In fact, the longshore members of the two locals are fairly even, with the excess of the white local being dock bosses, warehouse supervisors, and other such personnel who have retained membership in Local 1235. As they retire, more and more blacks succeed to their positions.[141]

On the New Jersey piers outside of Newark and located in Bayonne, Hoboken, and Jersey City, work is depressed because of the small number of arriving ships. There are white and black locals present, but the whites have greater numbers, seniority, and control a majority of the work that is available. In all New Jersey longshore work, gangs are not racially mixed. On occasion, there have been black foremen of white gangs or white foremen of black

---

Marseilles, Wertheim Publications in Industrial Relations (Cambridge: Harvard University Press, 1964), pp. 79-80.

140. *Ibid.,* p. 80; and Jensen, *Strife on the Waterfront . . ., op. cit.,* p. 27.

141. Information on the New Jersey situation is based on interviews and correspondence, with company, union, and Waterfront Commission Officials, June, November, and December 1973, and January 1974.

TABLE 13. *Longshore Industry*
Employment by Race and Occupational Group
New Jersey, 1966, 1969, 1970 [a]

Occupational Group	1966			1969			1970		
	Total [b]	Negro	Percent Negro	Total [b]	Negro	Percent Negro	Total [b]	Negro	Percent Negro
Officials and managers	31	—	—	187	4	2.1	137	4	2.9
Professionals	2	—	—	16	—	—	11	—	—
Technicians	—	—	—	23	4	17.4	35	1	2.9
Sales workers	1	—	—	16	—	—	11	—	—
Office and clerical	183	1	0.5	117	4	3.4	82	5	6.1
Total white collar	217	1	0.5	359	12	3.3	276	10	3.6
Craftsmen	102	38	37.3	138	19	13.8	172	14	8.1
Operatives	—	—	—	760	166	21.8	637	221	34.7
Laborers	1,236	426	34.5	842	517	61.4	55	34	61.8
Service workers	—	—	—	27	3	11.1	16	3	18.8
Total blue collar	1,338	464	34.7	1,767	705	39.9	880	272	30.9
Total	1,555	465	29.9	2,126	717	33.7	1,156	282	24.4

Source: U.S. Equal Employment Opportunity Commission, 1966, 1969, 1970.

[a] These data cover 5 establishments in 1966, 9 establishments in 1969, and 7 establishments in 1970.

[b] Includes males and females, although the number of females in the industry is small.

gangs, however, such combinations are never in effect for more than a day at a time.

The shift to containerization has arrested somewhat the decline in employment in Brooklyn. Areas which were deteriorating have been rehabilitated by the construction of new container facilities, and this has increased shipping calls. One major local, 1814, controls all the work on the Brooklyn docks. This local is dominated by Italian-Americans, although 10 percent of its 7,000 members are black. These blacks joined when their all-black local, 968, merged with 1814 in 1958. The gangs in Brooklyn are not racially mixed and blacks there have complained that they have not received a fair share of overtime ("golden hour") work. The waterfront commission has brought charges against some employers as a result which allegedly has improved the situation. Part of the problem appears to originate with the employers and hiring bosses themselves who are of Italian descent and tend to favor their own ethnic group, or are pressured into doing so.[142]

Passenger Liner Work and Its Decline

For years the "cream" of the jobs for New York longshoremen was the passenger liner dockings in mid-Manhattan. On the whole, the work was relatively pleasant and the men received tips for carrying passenger baggage. The Irish have always dominated this work; Local 824, which controlled piers 84 to 97, as late as 1964 had only one Negro among its 2,000 members. Another, Local 1811, which controlled piers 64 to 74 south of the luxury liner berths where some passenger ships other than the large luxury liners dock, had 300 blacks among its 500 members.

After years of agitation by various black civil rights groups and numerous charges before New York antidiscrimination agencies, Local 824 agreed to accept a merger with 1811. The merger was also discussed with locals in lower Manhattan, but failed to materialize because of the decline of both shipping and jobs in that area.[143]

---

142. Interviews with officials of Local 1814, Brooklyn, New York, and with those of Waterfront Commission of New York Harbor, June 1973. See also *The Brooklyn Longsoremen* (organ of Local 1814), June and August 1972, for stories on Brooklyn waterfront rehabilitation.

143. See "Two Dock Unions Plan Integration," *New York Times*, September 13, 1963; and "2 Locals Shelve Merger in I.L.A.," *ibid.*, September 17, 1963.

In the following years, the question became academic because the jet engine driven airplane effectively put the luxury liners, and most others except the cruise ships, out of business. Today the luxury liner piers are used for storage and parking. The white longshoremen who monopolized this work are still being paid just to report for work under the longshore guaranteed employment plan.

Clerks, Checkers, and Hiring Bosses

As has been the case throughout the country, clerks and checkers in the Port of New York have, until recently, traditionally been all white. All clerks and checkers throughout the port are members of Local No. 1, which has been headed for many years by Thomas W. (Teddy) Gleason, who is also currently president of the ILA. Local No. 1 was one of the most exclusive prior to litigation which forced it to open its doors to blacks.

This litigation began in 1957, when a series of complaints were filed before the New York State Commission Against Discrimination (now the New York State Human Relations Division) charging Local No. 1 with excluding blacks. On June 1, 1959, the local, through Mr. Gleason, agreed to a consent stipulation, ordering the admission of two blacks to membership, and agreed to consider others without discrimination. It was also stipulated that if Local No. 1 could not fully comply with all the terms to the commissions' satisfaction, it might enter an order against Local No. 1 embodying the stipulated terms.

When the union did not comply, the Commission obtained an order of enforcement from the New York state courts in May 1961. Local No. 1 did not purge itself of discrimination by the following March, the state commission obtained from the same court a show cause order in order to explain why Mr. Gleason and the local should not be held in contempt of court. Finally on October 22, 1962, after two additional court hearings, Local No. 1 satisfied the commission that it was complying with the court order, and the case was dismissed.[144]

---

144. *State Commission Against Discrimination* v. *Checkers and Clerks Union Local No. 1, ILA*, New York State Commission Against Discrimination, June 1, 1959, Complaint Case No. C-4750-57; New York Supreme Court, New York County, May 1, 1961 and April 27, 1962, No. 40508/1961; Special Terms, Part 1, October 22, 1962. 4 Race Relations Law Reporter 804 (1959); 7 Race Relations Law Reporter 492 (1962); 8 Race Relations Law Reporter 164 (1963).

Although the New York State antidiscrimination commission opened Local No. 1's doors, it was the policies of the Waterfront Commission of New York Harbor and the power of the New Jersey ILA black local (No. 1233) which has permitted increased numbers of minorities to become checkers. In 1968, the waterfront commission announced that the demand for new checkers would be filled by applicants who were longshoremen, and if there were more applicants than the 150 job openings available, checkers who qualified would be assigned on the basis of their seniority as longshoremen.[145] Resulting from this and other action, an estimated 100 of the 3,000 members of Local No. 1 are now black or Puerto Rican.[146] The bulk of the minority checkers are in the Newark, New Jersey, area, where the leadership of the black local, No. 1233, has insisted that its members would "not put up with" an all-white checker labor force.

The hiring bosses or agents are almost always white, although perhaps five or six blacks have gained this key position. The lack of blacks in this function and the propensity of such bosses to favor their own ethnic groups tends to react against black employment. The black gangs, as already noted, have black foremen.

New York—Final Comment

Given the fact that blacks are well represented in the expansion area of the Port of New York, they should continue to share in the work there. Overall, however, this great port is declining in its share of business because of its high-cost position. One of those key costs is the Guaranteed Annual Income Plan which, according to an official of the waterfront commission, costs shippers through the Port of New York, $2.30 per ton of cargo.[147] Other ports pay out very little, but New York is in effect supporting several thousand nonworking longshoremen, many of whom hold other jobs, but may still receive up to $10,000 per year for "badging in" —reporting to work. Ironically, a large number of these well paid nonworkers are the Manhattan longshoremen who kept blacks out of the better jobs for so long, and now inflict a cost which may well

145. "150 Checker Jobs Open to Dockers," *New York Times*, March 4, 1968. Also interviews and correspondence, June and November 1973.

146. Interviews, July and November 1973.

147. See Jensen, *Strife on the Waterfront . . .* , *op. cit.*, pp. 317-341, for an account of the excess which have developed relating to the Guaranteed Annual Income plan (GAI).

inhibit an expansion of job opportunities for blacks and whites alike.

PHILADELPHIA

The Port of Philadelphia, which is the hub of the Delaware Valley waterfront activity, represents an atypical situation in relation to other northeastern ports in so far as blacks are concerned. The port makes a substantial contribution to the economy of the Delaware Valley; approximately one in every ten jobs in manufacturing, and the wholesale and retail trades depends upon materials and merchandise passing through the port.[148] There is claimed to be a total of 55,300 port dependent jobs of which approximately 25,600 are nongovernment maritime activities, including shipping, cargo handling, shipbuilding, and repair.[149]

The following section will attempt to describe the growing role of the Negro, who has been in the majority on the waterfront for many years and the development of their influential black union leadership.

Pre-1900 Longshoremen

There is relatively little in the literature concerning pre-1900 longshoring in Philadelphia and even less concerning black waterfront workers. There is on record, however, the fact that in 1779 a group of Philadelphia seamen who worked as part-time longshoremen, struck for higher wages.[150] The racial composition of the seamen at this time is unknown, nor is it known whether the strikers belonged to a formal organization. As already noted, Philadelphia longshoremen joined in the New York strike of 1836, producing the first coastwise longshore incident. There is no record of a viable organization of longshoremen around this time, nor is it known whether any blacks participated in the strike in Philadelphia. According to Russell, "[i]n New York, Philadelphia, and Boston there were attempts at primitive collective bargaining and occasional group refusals to work in the very early 1800's, but not until 1836 were any facts of a work stoppage actually printed."[151]

---

148. Delaware River Port Authority, *The Economic Impact of the Delaware River Ports* (Philadelphia: n.d.), p. 2.

149. *Ibid.*, pp. 18-19.

150. Russell, *op. cit.*, p. 248.

151. *Ibid.*, pp. 12-13.

Russell goes on to note that the Knights of Labor met with success, organizing the Philadelphia waterfront in the very early 1880's and that the terrorist "Molly Maguires" gained a following of Philadelphia longshoremen in the late 1870's.[152] Unfortunately, Russell provides no information relative to black longshoremen during this period.

There is some evidence to indicate that blacks may have been involved in union organization during the 1890-1900 period. According to W. E. B. Du Bois, in 1896 there were 164 Negro longshoremen residing in Philadelphia, representing approximately 2.5 percent of all Negroes gainfully employed and living in the seventh ward.[153] At approximately the same time, Edward McHugh, a British trade unionist, was meeting with success in his attempts to organize Philadelphia and New York longshoremen.[154] Since McHugh operated his union until 1898, it is possible that black longshoremen in Philadelphia participated as members or at least were affected by the organization. Whatever gains the McHugh organization achieved, however, were shortlived and Northrup notes that 19th century longshore unions in Philadelphia were all destroyed before 1900.[155]

1900 to World War I—the IWW

Although the ILA began organizational efforts in the Port of Philadelphia in 1909, the longshoremen remained unorganized until 1913. At that time, the dockworkers went out on strike and soon after voted to affiliate with the Marine Transport Workers of the Industrial Workers of the World (IWW), rather than the ILA.[156] It has been estimated that more than one-half of the membership was Negro—2,200 of 4,200 longshoremen.[157] This estimate lends substantial credence to the hypothesis that blacks gained early admittance to the Philadelphia waterfront and may have achieved majority status before World War I and its con-

---

152. *Ibid.*, pp. 18-20.

153. W. E. Burghardt Du Bois, *The Philadelphia Negro* (Philadelphia: University of Pennsylvania, 1899), pp. 101, 108.

154. Russell, *op. cit.*, pp. 48-50.

155. Northrup, *op. cit.*, p. 144.

156. Spero and Harris, *op. cit.*, p. 111; and Northrup, *loc. cit.*

157. Spero and Harris, *loc. cit.*

comitant labor shortage. Census data for the 1910-1920 period provide further evidence (see Table 14). Although the data in Table 14 reflect employment in the entire state of Pennsylvania, the majority of longshoremen work on the Philadelphia piers where the black percentage is probably higher than is reflected in state-wide employment. In any event, between 1910 and 1920, blacks increased their percentage of longshore jobs by approximately 17 percentage points. More important is that the census data, which probably understate the extent of employment, indicate that as early as 1910, before organization by the IWW, blacks held a substantial number of longshore jobs in Pennsylvania longshoring.

Although the IWW was a revolutionary organization, the Marine Transport Workers union was operated along strict business lines, with the membership remaining quite patriotic during World War I.[158] The Marine Transport Workers differentiated itself from other labor organizations along racial lines and "managed to bring white men and black men into one organization in which race distinctions were obliterated in both the leadership and the rank and file." [159] This organizational policy was carried forward into the ILA, which gained control of the Philadelphia waterfront in the 1920's.[160]

The downfall of the IWW came "after 1920 [when] the Communists won control of the Philadelphia longshoremen and destroyed their union by a series of ill-timed strikes. The ILA fell heir to the remnants and has since completed the organization of the port." [161] It is important to remember, however, that the black members of the Marine Transport Workers local of the IWW ". . . were loyal unionists who would strike, hit the picket line, or go to jail as willingly as any white member. . . . [T]his loyalty was determined by purely practical consideration." [162]

1930 to the Present

In 1932, Boris Stern noted that

[t]here are from 4,000 to 5,000 longshoremen in the port of Philadelphia, of whom about 2,500 are organized in one local of the International Long-

---

158. Russell, *op. cit.*, p. 91.

159. Northrup, *op. cit.*, p. 144.

160. *Ibid.*

161. *Ibid.*

162. Spero and Harris, *op. cit.*, p. 112.

TABLE 14. *Longshore Industry*
Total and Negro Employment
Pennsylvania, 1910-1970

	1910	1920	1930	1940	1950	1960	1970
Total	3,522	4,224	4,345	3,273	3,152	2,156	1,634
Negro	1,428	2,409	2,252	1,342	1,502	1,120	843
Percent Negro	40.5	57.0	51.8	41.0	47.7	51.9	51.6

Source: Tables 5, 6, 7, pp. 41, 42, 44.

shoremen's Association. The membership is fairly evenly divided between colored and white, the white workers being predominantly Polish or of other Slavac nationalities.[163]

The number of Negroes in the local, therefore, was approximately 1,200 or somewhat more than one-half of all Negroes in the industry in Pennsylvania for 1930 (see Table 14).

In contrast, one local authority notes that prior to World War II, and for some time during the war, the two largest longshore locals, 1291 and 1332, were each 70 percent white.[164] This same authority contends that the severe labor shortage occasioned by World War II and the unskilled-semiskilled nature of longshore work opened the Philadelphia waterfront to blacks in the early 1940's and not earlier. The census data in Table 14 and the arguments of such noted authorities as Spero and Harris, Northrup, and Stern present clear evidence that black participation in Philadelphia longshoring reached significant proportions first in the 1900-1920 period and not during World War II.

Local 1291, the largest in the port, operated without regard to racial distinctions. According to Northrup, "[w]hite and colored workers work[ed] together, often in the same gangs, and are members of the same locals. One hears few complaints among Negroes that they are denied work because of their race. . . ."[165] This local, however, has not remained entirely clear of racial difficulties. Since its beginnings, Local 1291's by-laws required that the local president must be black, the vice president must be white, the recording secretary must be white, the financial secretary must be black, and other minor officials must be equally apportioned between the races.[166] Beginning in the mid-1960's, these provisions have been attacked in the courts as denying individual union members of their rights to nominate for office candidates of their own choosing or to hold office themselves.[167] In essence, the complaints alleged violations of the Landrum-Griffin Act of 1959. After approximately eight

163. Boris Stern, *Cargo Handling and Longshore Labor Conditions*, Bulletin No. 550 (Washington: U.S. Bureau of Labor Statistics, 1932), p. 83.

164. Interview, July 3, 1973.

165. Northrup, *op. cit.*, p. 143.

166. *Shultz* v. *Local 1291, International Longshoremen's Ass'n,* 338 F. Supp. 1205 (1972).

167. 338 F. Supp. at 1204-1208.

years of litigation the courts have upheld the argument declaring void a 1964 election, but it is rather doubtful that the weight of the court decision will reverse the trends developed through years of black control and the traditional ties developed on the docks. The current president, Richard Askew, a black, has served in his office for many years and appears to be in firm control of the local.[168]

Table 15 presents the approximate number of blacks in the various Philadelphia longshore locals in 1970. As can be seen, the two locals engaged in actual loading and unloading operations, Locals 1291 and 1332, are predominantly black. On the other hand, the clerks and checkers local, 1242, is almost entirely white. These "white collar" occupations in the industry have traditionally been controlled by white workers throughout the country, and apparently, Philadelphia is no exception. In 1965, Professor Marshall reported that during the 1953-1956 period:

> In Philadelphia, [a President's Committee on Government Contracts] investigation revealed that employers wanted to hire Negroes as weighers and checkers, but were prevented from doing so by an International Longshoremen's Association (ILA) local in that city. In one case a company became involved in a dispute with the ILA when it attempted to hire Negro checkers. The dispute was settled when the union agreed that Negroes could work "up the hook" but all other jobs would have to be filled through the ILA.[169]

As late as 1966, the Philadelphia Commission on Human Relations found that the 275 members of Local 1242, Clerks and Checkers, were all white. Although ". . . the union had a list of prospective Negro employees, . . . Negroes were never hired because they were not union members."[170] The Commission issued an order instructing employers to hire Negro clerks and checkers, however the data in Table 15 indicate that only minor changes had occurred four years after the Commission's decision.

In summation, it appears that the Philadelphia waterfront has offered job opportunities for blacks in significant numbers

---

168. Efforts to interview Mr. Askew for this study met with no success.

169. Ray Marshall, *The Negro and Organized Labor* (New York: John Wiley & Sons, Inc., 1965), p. 222. Presumably, the ILA local was 1242.

170. Orrin Evans, "Stevedores Told to Hire Negro Clerks," *Philadelphia Evening Bulletin*, Oct. 4, 1966.

TABLE 15. *Longshore Industry*
Estimated Negro Membership in Philadelphia Longshore Locals
1970

Local		Total	Negro	Percent Negro
1291	Longshoremen	2,200	1,430	65.0
1332	Carloaders	650	585	90.0
1566	Cleaners and Carpenters	185	92	49.7
1242	Clerks and Checkers	507	11	2.2
1242-1	Timekeepers	30	—	—

Source: Field interviews, October 2, 1970.

as far back as the World War I period. In addition, the union structure, including both the IWW and ILA, has allowed for the development of influential black leaders and for relatively few instances of racial difficulties. Mixed gangs and mixed local membership have been the rule, rather than the exception, in this port. But, on the other hand, little progress has been made in opening skilled white collar clerk and checker positions to blacks.

BALTIMORE

The Port of Baltimore has always been one of the larger ports in the country in terms of tonnage handled, and has always been a leading employer of Negro longshoremen. The maritime industries have flourished in Baltimore since 1736, one year after the city was founded,[171] providing shipbuilding, cargo handling, and offshore maritime job opportunities for both black and white Baltimore residents. As will be detailed below, the Port of Baltimore, as in most southern ports, was organized in such a way as to permit not only many longshore jobs for Negroes but also to allow for the development of strong and influential Negro union leaders. Nevertheless, racial discrimination still flourished.

1800 to 1920

Although many blacks probably worked on the Baltimore waterfront during the first half of the nineteenth century, as

171. Russell, *op. cit.*, p. 252.

did Frederick Douglass between 1825 and 1832,[172] it was not until the 1870's that the number of Negro longshoremen became large enough for them to form a labor organization.

> The effect of the organization of Negro labor upon labor conditions was the same as among white workingmen. There is one instance during this period in which an organization secured an increase of wages by its united action. On June 26, 1871, the longshoremen of Baltimore met and organized the Longshoremen's Association No. 1, and it was proposed to incorporate it with the National Labor Union.[173]

This organization was all-black and, ironically, its success may have provided the impetus for the removal of Negroes from the waterfront. Coupled with an increasing rate of immigration, the desire of the predominantly German longshoremen to deprive the Negro of longshore work met with success, thereby displacing most Negroes by 1900.[174]

The removal of blacks, however, did not last very long.

> [In 1900] the German workers, the largest group in the port, led a strike against Sunday work. One of the firms involved imported a body of Negroes from its docks at Norfolk, and used them to check the walkout. From then on the number of Negro longshoremen increased. Many of the stevedores preferred them to white workers because "you can tell them what to do and they'll do it." [175]

According to Northrup, the black majority on the Baltimore waterfront that developed before World War I can be traced directly to the 1916 strike and the introduction of the Negro as a strikebreaker.[176] It is probable that the ILA was involved in this strike since its organizational efforts in the port began in 1900, but it was not until 1912 that the current ILA organization was created.[177]

The importance of the Negro to the Baltimore longshore industry can be gauged from a comment by Greene and Woodson who noted that at the turn of the century, border city longshor-

172. *Ibid.*, p. 253.

173. Wesley, *op. cit.*, p. 184.

174. Northrup, *op. cit.*, p. 144.

175. Spero and Harris, *op. cit.*, p. 192.

176. Northrup, *op. cit.*, p. 145.

177. *Ibid.*, p. 144.

ing was becoming more and more divided between the races.[178] Greene's and Woodson's source material for this statement was a study of Negroes in Maryland after the Civil War and, therefore, must have included the Port of Baltimore. Greene and Woodson went on to note that around 1915 "[a]nother large railroad brought 10,000 Negroes from the Baltimore docks and distributed them in railroad camps along its line in Philadelphia, Pittsburgh, Cincinnati, and other cities." [179]

The data in Table 16 clearly indicate that the availability of 10,000 Negroes from the Baltimore waterfront must have been a serious overestimate. It is important to note, however, that the use of black Baltimore longshoremen in other parts of the country implied that there was an excess of Negroes on the Baltimore docks. The data in Table 16 support this hypothesis by noting a large black majority in Maryland longshoring during the 1910-1920 period.

The Rise of the ILA

According to Russell the city's longshore industry was "[o]rganized by the ILA in the early 1900's with both white and Negro locals in the port (the Negro were larger and more active), Baltimore's longshore unions had erratic careers. Both the ILA and the Industrial Workers of the World ("Wobblies") were on the docks of Baltimore during World War I, but by 1917 the ILA had practical control." [180] Initially, Negroes and whites were organized into mixed locals, but disagreements led to separate charters being granted to black longshoremen.[181] As a result, most of the Negroes handling freight on ships and on the docks were under ILA jurisdiction. Some hostility between Negroes and the union remained, however, as a result of Negroes being refused work on the all-white railroad piers. This exclusion was primarily responsible for the use of Negro strikebreakers on these piers in 1916 and the open acceptance of the Marine Transport Workers, IWW, during the same year.[182] The

178. Greene and Woodson, *op. cit.*, p. 114.

179. *Ibid.*, p. 266.

180. Russell, *op. cit.*, p. 83.

181. Spero and Harris, *loc. cit.*

182. *Ibid.*, p. 193.

TABLE 16. *Longshore Industry*
Total and Negro Employment
Maryland, 1910-1970

	1910	1920	1930	1940	1950	1960	1970
Total	2,975	4,349	3,400	3,359	3,445	2,117	1,756
Negro	1,933	3,179	2,334	2,016	2,314	1,248	980
Percent Negro	65.0	73.1	68.6	60.0	67.2	59.0	55.8

Source: Tables 5, 6, 7, pp. 41, 42, 44.

1916 strike paved the way for continued Negro employment on the railroad piers, but it was not until 1933 that they joined the union.[183] The IWW disappeared soon after World War I. Two locals, 829 and 858, received their charters in 1913 and 1914 respectively and since that time Local 829 has remained all-white and Local 858 has remained all-black. This occurrence led to a major court case that will be discussed below.

1930 to 1960

The census data in Table 16 show that blacks continued to be in the majority during the 1930-1960 period. By 1940, the port achieved a partial decasualized arrangement as the unions limited membership by means of high initiation fees and "exacting port regulations" kept stragglers off the docks. Work was supposed to be divided evenly between the white and black locals, but blacks apparently received a disproportionate share of disagreeable or difficult cargoes.[184] Moreover, since there were more Negroes than whites in their respective locals, an even division of work between the locals in fact discriminated against the black longshoremen. Yet, as the following quotation illustrates, this basic unfairness frequently went unnoticed:

> When a new local was formed in the racially troubled city of Cambridge, Maryland, [ILA President] Teddy Gleason, hearing reports of possible difficulties, went immediately to the port. . . . The ILA President told all parties flatly and finally that the fair—and integrated—agreement that prevailed in Baltimore would also apply to Cambridge. Both sides could accept it on the spot, or expect the entire strength of the waterfront union to oppose them. The dispute, the segregation, and the brewing mass demonstration ended then and there.[185]

Because of the unfair work division between the Baltimore locals and the large proportion of disagreeable and difficult cargo handled by blacks, it is hard to see where the Baltimore agreement is "fair-and-integrated."

It was, nevertheless, incidents such as the above that in 1966 prompted Russell, in her official history of the ILA, to state:

> The Port [of Baltimore] is an outstanding example of interracial co-operation and achievement. In 1892 the ILA's constitution declared, "We

183. Northrup, *op. cit.*, p. 145.

184. *Ibid.*, pp. 144-145.

185. Russell, *op. cit.*, p. 237.

recognize that ability makes the man and not wealth or social distinction. We recognize no nationality or creed. . . ." On the Baltimore docks this principle has become daily practice. While perfection may not have been attained, the longshore unions of the city have handled minority problems with intelligence, sanity, and good will.[186]

However, the ensuing events make unclear whether Russell's observation was correct. In fact, a longshore local president from Brooklyn disagreed with Russell long before the government took issue with the Baltimore situation. According to the official Local 1814, Brooklyn, membership report, ". . . segregation lies at the core of many of the ILA's problems; and . . . that until the ILA rids itself of segregation, it will remain split on many vital issues. . . ."[187] The ILA official was ahead of his time in his call for a merger between locals 829 and 858, just as he was premature in noting that there would be solid resistance to the merger from both the leaders of all-black Local 858 and 858 rank-and-file. It is quite understandable that Negro union officials would be resistant to changes that could erode the control over job opportunities and the status they had achieved over time. Although the amount of work and kinds of work done by Local 858 may not have been optimal, as it might be under full integration, it was certainly predictable and under the direct control of Negroes, and for Negroes. Merger and integration carried too many uncertainties and potentially damaging alterations in work rules and practices for Negro leaders of Local 858 to be in favor of them.

Government Pressure for Merger

The federal government declared that segregated locals, segregated hiring halls, segregated gangs, and disproportionate work sharing were all counter to current civil rights policy and sued for their removal.[188] In the complaint, the government alleged that the above practices resulted in less total work, less desirable work, and lower total earnings for Negroes. Included in the requested relief was a complete merger of seniority lines and

186. *Ibid.*, p. 253.

187. ILA, Local 1814, "Report to the Membership," October 11, 1966, p. 1. These observations concerning the Baltimore situation were made after a first-hand visit by Anthony Scotto, President, Local 1814.

188. *United States* v. *International Longshoremen's Ass'n*, 319 F. Supp. 737 (D.C. Md. 1970).

gangs to be accomplished by a daily shape-up or a one-time reformation of all gangs, many of which had been working together for 10 or 20 years.

As was expected, opposition to complete change was voiced from both white and black locals but especially noteworthy was the reaction of leadership of the black local, No. 858. The president, William Haile, went on public record as being against the merger fearing a loss of influence, domination by the white leadership in the ILA, and a loss of efficiency and safety precautions should the gang structure be altered.[189]

The union's defense to the suit included four major points. First, separate charters were issued to black locals to protect them and to insure that they receive 50 percent of all available work. Secondly, Local 829 has always had some Negro members and Local 858 has always had some white members, recently admitting 250 more blacks. Thirdly, there are no union consitiutional provisions allowing for discrimination; and lastly, member's freedom of association rights would be abridged if a merger took place.[190] In addition, the union contended that the existing gang system was a more productive and safer method of operation than that proposed by the government. The primary reason for this is that "a gang working together every day operates as a team and the men get to know each other's method of work." [191] Finally, the union argued that the disporportionate number of hours worked between the two locals can be accounted for by the fact that mechanics, gearmen, and foremen all belong to Local 829 and that the union has little influence over company choice of these men.[192]

In essence, the district court ruled in favor of the government on all counts except the merging of all gangs. The underlying conclusion of the court was that "the maintenance of locals whose membership is segregated by race is a *per se* violation of Section 703(c)(2) of the [1964 Civil Rights]

---

189. *Baltimore Sun,* September 3, 1970.

190. See generally brief for Defendant, "Proposed Findings of Facts and Conclusions of Law," *United States* v. *International Longshoremen's Ass'n,* 319 F. Supp. 737 (D.C. Md. 1970).

191. *Ibid.,* p. 5.

192. *Ibid.,* pp. 6-7.

Act."[193] The court ruled that it was not necessary to show that unequal job opportunities do exist, but only that the system would tend to deprive any individual of employment opportunities.[194] In practical terms, the court ordered that the locals be merged, that one hiring hall be maintained, and that seniority lines be merged,[195] arguing that this relief would tend to aid rather than hinder efficiency. The court refused, however, to order a merging of the gangs accepting the union argument that efficiency and safety would be jeopardized if the government's petition was accepted, citing as evidence the excellent safety rate of Baltimore, where gangs have remained intact for quite some time, as compared to other ports, where gangs are formed on a daily basis.[196]

The district court order contained a stay of execution pending an appeal. The result of the appeal, however, was a confirmation in entirety of the lower court ruling.[197] Only one of the three-judge panel dissented, in part, holding that a single hiring hall would accomplish all that the government requested and that merger of the two locals would, therefore, be unnecessary. In November 1972, the U.S. Supreme Court denied *certiorari* ordering that the prior lower court ruling be put into effect within 60 to 90 days.[198]

After some delay, a consent decree was signed on May 31, 1973 effectuating the merger. At present, there exists one local, 333, with dual office holding, merged seniority lines, one hiring hall for general longshoremen, and gangs remain segregated.

It is too early to determine what will be the impact of the case on black employment. It may well be that, as a result of their numerical superiority, blacks will take over control of the merged local and increase their job participation in the port. There is a tendency for whites to look elsewhere than on the docks for work, and the merger could increase this tendency. At the present time, leadership jobs in the merged

193. 319 F. Supp. at 743-744.

194. *Ibid.* at 744.

195. *Ibid.* at 748-749.

196. *Ibid.* at 750-751.

197. 460 F.2d 497 (4th Cir. 1972).

198. 409 U.S. 1007 (1972).

local are divided between blacks and whites, and gangs are rotated so as to give both races a fair and reasonable opportunity on both quantity and quality of jobs.

The court found that Negroes had been discriminated against by being virtually excluded from jobs such as mechanics, gearmen, and foremen, and it ordered an end to this practice. Curiously, the case did not involve clerks and checkers, who have been traditionally white and remain so in the Port of Baltimore. Why the federal government did not pursue this inequality, which is easily demonstrable to be more invidious than the other discriminatory features to which it objected, is difficult to understand.

HAMPTON ROADS

The Hampton Roads district of Virginia includes the ports of Newport News, Norfolk, and Portsmouth. The ports lie at the mouth of the Chesapeake Bay where several rivers and the Atlantic Ocean merge. The location is ideal for waterborne commerce and, as such, for the development of a longshore industry. More important, however, is that the growth of waterborne commerce in Hampton Roads has meant the growth of, and almost complete control of, waterfront job opportunities for black longshoremen.

Negroes and Unions: 1880 to World War I

Although Richmond, Virginia, is almost 100 miles up the James River from the Hampton Roads district, "[t]here was reported a stevedores' strike [there] on May 4, 1867; mention of another such at City Point [Hopewell] appeared May 2, 1869. . . ."[199] These incidents supply evidence that Virginia longshoremen, like dockworkers in other ports, were among the first groups of workers to seek economic betterment through labor organizations. It is reasonable to conclude also that blacks were involved in the Richmond and City Point incidents since most of the longshore work in the Hampton Roads area, at the mouth of the James River, was done by Negroes.[200] However, the actual racial composition of these organizations and how long they survived is not known.

---

199. A. A. Taylor, *The Negro in the Reconstruction of Virginia* (1924; reprint ed., New York: Russell and Russell, 1969), p. 120.

200. See below for corroboration.

The influence of black longshoremen in these ports can be seen during ". . . the peak year of labor of 1886, while Negro longshoremen of Norfolk, Virginia were striking for an increase of five cents an hour, fifty white strikebreakers were imported from New York."[201] The use of white strikebreakers against Negro laborers represents an atypical situation and lends credence to the notion that when the Knights of Labor organized the Virginia waterfront, they organized the controlling black longshoremen.

It is known that the Knights of Labor remained active in Hampton Roads during the early 1890's and that the ILA had organized a few all-black locals at Newport News prior to 1900.[202] "In 1899 . . . [t]he local unions [of Newport News longshoremen] were composed of Negroes and the whites refused to join them. The question was settled by the issuance of a separate charter to the white workers."[203] The white and Negro longshoremen entered into an agreement whereby all available longshore work would be divided among the races.[204] According to Greene and Woodson, it was between 1890 and 1910 that many Negro longshore jobs in the South were being taken over by whites.[205] This corresponds directly to the period of organization by the Knights of Labor. According to Russell, however, southern longshoring became a black and white occupation during the Reconstruction when the supply of labor was quite high and wages quite low.[206] Russell also notes that southern waterfront employers made frequent trips to Europe to entice immigration to southern docks, but they met with no success.[207] This can be contrasted to the northern situation where the influx of Italian workers helped to ease the domination of the Irish over the waterfront.

---

201. Sidney H. Kessler, "The Organization of Negroes in the Knights of Labor," in John H. Bracey *et al., Black Workers and Organized Labor* (Belmont, Calif.: Wadsworth Publishing Co., Inc., 1971), p. 7.

202. Northrup, *op. cit.,* p. 146.

203. Wesley, *op. cit.,* pp. 258-259.

204. Northrup, *loc. cit.*

205. Greene and Woodson, *op. cit.,* p. 133.

206. Russell, *op. cit.,* p. 45.

207. *Ibid.*

Although there were ILA locals in Hampton Roads prior to 1908,[208] the present day ILA structure began in 1912 when the Negro coal trimmers of Hampton Roads met in secret and formed a labor organization,[209] the Coal Trimmers' Union. This organization, which had been preceded by the formation of the Transportation Workers Association of Virginia (TWA) in 1910, composed of Negro longshoremen in Norfolk, was chartered by the AFL as a federal labor union.[210] The coal trimmers did not affiliate with the ILA until World War I. Interestingly, Spero and Harris noted that around this time, the general longshoremen's union in the ILA at Newport News had no Negro members. Black longshoremen there had formed an independent union which came into the ILA in 1917.[211]

1920 to the Present

The rise of union strength in Hampton Roads, and the growing influence of black union leaders, continued through World War I and for sometime thereafter. In 1921, the Negro coal trimmers strike was opposed by the black union leadership; however, despite the use of white strikebreakers by the employers, higher wages were won.[212]

During the height of World War I, the entire 8,000 to 9,000 man Hampton Roads waterfront work force was organized. Of these, at least 6,000 were Negro.[213]

After the war union strength declined rapidly. . . . Today [1931] of about six thousand men employed in the district, 2,200 are organized. Of approximately 4,000 unorganized workers, about 500 are white and 3,500 black. Of the organized workers about 200 are white and about 2,000 colored. The colored worker thus dominates union affairs in the district. Of the nine locals seven are black and two white. There are no mixed locals due, first, to the strength of the southern tradition of racial segre-

---

208. *Ibid.*, p. 83.

209. *Ibid.*, p. 255.

210. Spero and Harris, *op. cit.*, pp. 195-196.

211. *Ibid.*, p. 196.

212. *Ibid.*, p. 195.

213. F. Ray Marshall, *Labor in the South* (Cambridge: Harvard University Press, 1967), p. 68.

gation and, second, to the preference of the Negroes themselves for their own organizations.[214]

The reason for the postwar decline in union membership can be attributed to the open shop movement during the 1920's that seriously weakened southern longshore unions[215] and the sharp cutbacks in employment resulting from increased mechanization introduced at Hampton Roads.[216] The leaders and the rank-and-file who remained organized, however, were predominantly black.

The downward trend did not continue very long, and according to Russell:

> During the first six years of the Roosevelt era, ILA membership soared upward at a rate surpassing even the remarkable organizational days of Dan Keefe. The South Atlantic and Gulf Coast District, for example [of which Hampton Roads is a part] had dwindled to a mere 3,000 members at the low point of the depression. Five years later, it had increased sixfold—18,000 union longshoremen worked in the District.[217]

The amount of increase occuring at Hampton Roads, however, may not have been as large as Russell thought. According to Northrup, ILA membership at Hampton Roads in August 1941 stood at approximately 2,700, including approximately 2,500 blacks.[218]

The data in Table 17 confirm both the decreasing size of the longshore work force in Virginia and the overwhelming dominance of black longshoremen. The black participation rate remained high throughout the period covered by the table. Although the participation rate fell below 90 percent in 1960 and 1970, some of the decline may be accounted for by census undercount as was noted for other areas. The important point to make, however, is that in periods of both increasing and decreasing employment, blacks remained in control of Virginia longshoring. Although the following quotation refers to a Brownsville, Texas, decision, the argument presented in it applies equally well to Hampton Roads.

---

214. As quoted in, *ibid.*, p. 68.

215. *Ibid.*, p. 202.

216. See Russell, *op. cit.*, p. 257; and Northrup, *op. cit.*, p. 146.

217. Russell, *op. cit.*, p. 126.

218. Northrup, *loc. cit.*

TABLE 17. *Longshore Industry*
Total and Negro Employment
Virginia, 1910-1970

	1910	1920	1930	1940	1950	1960	1970
Total	3,456	4,931	3,073	2,575	1,644	1,441	1,341
Negro	3,279	4,691	2,930	2,379	1,483	1,271	1,102
Percent Negro	94.9	95.1	95.3	92.4	90.2	88.2	82.2

Source: Tables 5, 6, 7, pp. 41, 42, 44.

In older unionized sectors like longshoring, Negroes have been able to perpetuate their hold on certain jobs because of racial quota systems. Although in 1964 the NLRB declared the longshoremen's racial quotas to be unfair labor practices, it is doubtful that the decision will seriously disturb the longshoremen's quota system. Negroes are sometimes disadvantaged compared to whites, but they have good jobs in the industry and a strong position within the international union, and unless something happens to change their attitudes, the overwhelming majority of Negro ILA leaders in the South will apparently support the prevailing job system.[219]

The initial opposition expressed by Negro leaders in Baltimore can be echoed by Hampton Roads longshoremen. "Whether or not Negroes oppose integration depends partly upon the effects of segregation on their economic opportunities. Some unions, like the . . . Longshoremen . . . feel that their economic opportunities would not be improved if they integrated because they have protected territories." [220] In Virginia, this now includes virtually all longshore jobs. Hence, the blacks' desire to retain local autonomy within the ILA structure would operate as a deterrent to the merger of racially separated locals. The data in Table 18 support the above conclusions.[221] As can be seen, the sum total of white collar positions is extremely small and it is probable that the clerks and checkers are included in this group. They represent one area where change could be beneficial to blacks. Negroes have always been excluded from the clerks and checkers position and have made little progress in reversing the historically white complexion of the trade in Virginia, or for that matter, in most ports.

On the other hand, the blue collar jobs, especially in the laborer category where the general longshoremen appear, are overwhelmingly black in Virginia. It is the power base of Negro officials, deriving from the domination of blacks in the union, that makes them oppose further integration or even to reach out for clerks and checkers jobs.

---

219. F. Ray Marshall, "The Negro in Southern Unions," in Julius Jacobson, ed., *The Negro and the American Labor Movement* (Garden City, N.Y.: Anchor Books, Inc., 1968), pp. 145-146.

220. F. Ray Marshall, "Union Racial Practices," in Herbert R. Northrup and Richard L. Rowan, eds., *The Negro and Employment Opportunity* (Ann Arbor: Bureau of Industrial Relations, University of Michigan, 1965), p. 171.

221. These data are not comparable with census material. They are used merely to indicate the division of the longshore work force.

TABLE 18. *Longshore Industry*
Employment by Race and Occupational Group
Virginia, 1966, 1969 [a]

Occupational Group	1966			1969		
	Total	Negro	Percent Negro	Total	Negro	Percent Negro
Officials and managers	74	22	29.7	39	2	5.1
Professionals	—	—	—	1	—	—
Technicians	2	—	—	—	—	—
Sales workers	—	—	—	—	—	—
Office and clerical	73	1	1.4	37	1	2.7
Total white collar	149	23	15.4	77	3	3.9
Craftsmen	47	17	36.2	29	6	20.7
Operatives	80	55	68.8	6	2	33.3
Laborers	3,372	3,175	94.2	1,011	936	92.6
Service workers	—	—	—	—	—	—
Total blue collar	3,499	3,247	92.8	1,046	944	90.2
Total	3,648	3,270	89.6	1,123	947	84.3

Source: U.S. Equal Employment Opportunity Commission, 1966, 1969.

[a] These data cover 8 establishments in 1966 and 6 establishments in 1969.

SOUTH ATLANTIC

The South Atlantic ports in South Carolina, Georgia, and Florida have been traditional strongholds for Negro longshoremen and for Negro union organizations. In fact, some of the oldest locals in the current ILA structure originated in the South Atlantic region.

The Longshoremen's Protective Union Association, formed in Charleston, South Carolina, in 1867, was composed entirely of Negro longshoremen and represented "the most powerful organization of the colored laboring class in South Carolina." [222] "Eight years later, in 1875, the union had over eight hundred members and was able to gather five hundred for its parade. . . . Even at this time, a decade after the end of the Civil War, it had a long record of vigorously conducted strikes." [223]

Unfortunately, no information is available concerning the outcomes of the strikes, but it can be inferred that they were not total defeats since the union survived until at least 1875. It should be noted that this Charleston organization preceded the formation of the Negro longshore union in Baltimore by approximately five years and was probably more successful than the Baltimore group since increasing levels of German immigration into Baltimore eroded the strength of the black longshoremen there.

In 1874, a group of Negro longshoremen in Port Royal, South Carolina, followed the lead of the Charleston longshoremen and formed another union under the same title.[224] According to Tindall, both the Charleston and Port Royal groups survived into the late 1880's.[225] The strength of unions composed of Negro longshoremen in South Carolina can be seen in the fact that a strike in Charleston in 1890 led to the formation of a separate union of white dockworkers. The white longshoremen complained that waterfront disagreements were always settled in favor of Negroes.[226] The establishment of a white union,

---

222. Northrup, *op. cit.*, p. 147.

223. Spero and Harris, *op. cit.*, p. 183.

224. George B. Tindall, *South Carolina Negroes 1877-1900* (Baton Rouge: Louisiana State University Press, 1966), p. 137.

225. *Ibid.*

226. *Ibid.*, p. 138.

apparently, was an attempt to equalize the strength of the competing dockworkers. In summary, however, "it appears that Negroes virtually monopolized the stevedore work around the wharves in Charleston, Georgetown, and Beaufort." [227]

It is doubtful, however, that an organization of white longshoremen anywhere in South Carolina could have achieved any strength. The data for South Carolina in Table 19 indicate that blacks were in firm control of waterfront job opportunities for the entire time period covered by the table. During the World War I period (1910-1920) when the ILA became the dominant union in the area, blacks slightly increased their control over the developing waterfront.

The Georgia ports of Savannah and Brunswick have also been controlled by Negro longshoremen. Union activity in these ports parallels the development in Charleston, although the first organizations appeared around 1881. In that year, the Negro dock laborers in Savannah called a strike for higher wages that was met by the use of strikebreakers from Macon, violence erupted when local militia became involved in the dispute.[228] The name and formal structure of any labor union involved in the strike is not known, but it can be assumed that most, if not all, of the participants were black.

Further strikes occurred in 1885, 1887, 1889, 1891, and 1894. Most of them were over wage issues and most resulted in little or no gains for Negro longshoremen.[229] The Knights of Labor organized the Savannah and Brunswick Negro longshoremen during the early 1880's and apparently were involved in all the work stoppages. The ILA, according to most sources, entered the area in the 1890's.[230] According to Evans, however, an 1897 strike in both Savannah and Brunswick was a joint effort between the Knights of Labor and the ILA indicating that the ILA presence was felt in the area prior to 1899.[231] Virtually all historians agree that both the Knights of Labor

---

227. Taylor, *op. cit.*, p. 72.

228. Mercer G. Evans, "The History of the Organized Labor Movement In Georgia," unpublished Ph.D. dissertation, University of Chicago, 1929, p. 186 fn.

229. *Ibid.*, pp. 186-187.

230. See, for example, Northrup, *op. cit.*, p. 148.

231. Evans, *op. cit.*, pp. 188-190, fn. 6.

TABLE 19. *Longshore Industry*
Total and Negro Employment
South Carolina, Georgia, and Florida
1910-1970

State	1910	1920	1930	1940	1950	1960	1970
South Carolina							
Total	560	762	963	748	504	607	547
Negro	513	733	n.a.	729	479	583	524
Percent Negro	91.6	96.2	—	97.5	95.0	96.0	95.8
Georgia							
Total	1,762	1,799	1,608	1,353	687	787	672
Negro	1,683	1,680	1,554	1,308	657	744	564
Percent Negro	95.5	93.4	96.6	96.7	95.6	94.5	83.9
Florida							
Total	1,709	1,470	2,028	2,845	1,658	1,543	1,570
Negro	1,530	1,312	1,882	2,645	1,434	1,272	1,155
Percent Negro	89.5	89.3	92.8	93.0	86.5	82.4	73.6

Source: Tables 5, 6, 7, pp. 41, 42, 44.

and the ILA were overwhelmingly black. The data in Table 19 support this contention.

The ILA became the sole organizer of Georgia ports in 1910 by absorbing the remnants of the Knights of Labor. The organization continued to grow so that at the height of World War I, most of the Negro longshoremen were unionized. A defeated strike in 1921, however, saw the Brunswick local disappear entirely and the strength and influence of the Savannah group seriously weakened,[232] still the longshore work force remained largely black (see Table 19).

The strength of the ILA in Savannah was revived in 1936 [233] and since then, the ILA has dominated the waterfront. Again, all available census data indicate that blacks maintained an overwhelming majority on the waterfront. According to Marshall, the resurgence of the ILA led to the organization of every major port in the South and that by 1939, the ILA's southern membership stood at approximately 16,611.[234] It is reasonable to conclude that more than one-half of this total were Negro longshoremen.

The present day structure of both the longshore work force and the unions in the South Atlantic has changed very little since the 1930's. The data in Table 20, although not complete in coverage, clearly show that the actual work of longshoring (laborers and operatives) is done by blacks but most other occupations are filled by whites. The racial composition of the unions in the area provides further proof (see Figure 1). As can be seen, all of the longshore locals are black and all of the clerks and checkers groups are white. According to confidential sources, Savannah Local 1414 is entirely black except for four token white casuals and is expected to remain so in the future. In order for blacks to become clerks and checkers in Savannah, they would have to agree to relinquish some of the tight control they maintain over regular longshore employment and admit white longshoremen to the industry, however, the black leadership has been resistant to this change. Moreover, declining employment in these ports in recent years indicates that change will come slowly in the

232. *Ibid.*, p. 189.

233. Northrup, *op. cit.*, p. 148.

234. Marshall, *Labor in the South, op. cit.*, p. 211.

TABLE 20. *Longshore Industry*
Employment by Race and Occupational Group
South Carolina, Georgia, and Florida, 1966, 1969 [a]

Occupational Group	1966 [b]			1969		
	Total	Negro	Percent Negro	Total	Negro	Percent Negro
Officials and managers	188	25	13.3	170	21	12.4
Professionals	14	—	—	7	—	—
Technicians	—	—	—	1	—	—
Sales workers	16	—	—	1	—	—
Office and clerical	281	6	2.1	223	6	2.7
Total white collar	499	31	6.2	402	27	6.7
Craftsmen	70	1	1.4	28	2	7.1
Operatives	280	210	75.0	197	159	80.7
Laborers	1,719	1,618	94.1	2,432	2,205	90.7
Service workers	47	5	10.6	4	3	75.0
Total blue collar	2,116	1,834	86.7	2,661	2,369	89.0
Total	2,615	1,865	71.3	3,063	2,396	78.2

Source: U.S. Equal Employment Opportunity Commission, 1966, 1969.
[a] These data cover 14 establishments in 1966 and 15 establishments in 1969.
[b] Includes only Florida and Georgia.

FIGURE 1. *Longshore Industry*
Racial Composition and Jurisdiction of South Atlantic International Longshoremen's Association Locals, 1971

Location	Local No.	Race	Jurisdiction
Wilmington—Sunny Point, North Carolina	1426	Black	Longshore
	1838	Black	Longshore
	1776	White	Clerks and Checkers
Charleston, South Carolina	1422	Black	Longshore
	1771	White	Clerks and Checkers
Port Royal, South Carolina	1751	Black	Longshore
Georgetown, South Carolina	1861	Black	Longshore
Savannah, Georgia	1414	Black	Longshore
	1475	White	Clerks and Checkers
Jacksonville, Florida	1408	Black	Deepsea and Coastwise
	1408-A	Black	General Warehouse

Source: Data in author's possession.

future, regardless of the wishes of both parties. A major employer has advised the Industrial Research Unit that "work opportunity" has fallen off sufficiently causing ". . . considerable doubt that the present work force, even with natural attrition due to retirement, etc. can be maintained so there is little question of new employees entering the industry for years to come. In such circumstances there is little reason to expect any particular change in racial balance." [235]

NEW ORLEANS

The Port of New Orleans, near the mouth of the Mississippi River, serves the midcontinental United States, which contains 30 to 40 percent of the population, the purchasing power, and the productive industries of the United States. New Orleans ranks second only to New York in terms of the dollar value of foreign commerce and tonnage of total waterborne commerce. Waterfront employment in New Orleans has been a major source of economic opportunity for Negroes since the Civil War.

235. Letter, December 12, 1973; and interviews, Savannah, October 23, 1970.

1850-1900

According to Marshall, and Spero and Harris, blacks were introduced to the New Orleans waterfront as slaves during the Civil War and as free workers immediately following.[236] Strong union organization, however, came earlier when in 1850 a group of skilled waterfront workers formed the New Orleans Screwmen's Benevolent Association.[237] The screwmen were those skilled dock workers who, with the aid of jackscrews, compressed and stowed aboard ship more cotton bales than could otherwise be loaded. In turn, the exportation of cotton was made more profitable. These screwmen were originally all white.[238]

The success of the screwmen's union was almost immediate as their strategic location and skill, and therefore, tremendous bargaining power, allowed them to win wage gains totalling $3.50 more per day by 1866.[239] These gains were won, although the Civil War seriously depleted the screwmen's ranks.

According to Professor Northrup, black longshoremen, although engaging in strikes earlier, organized after the Civil War. "In 1872 the Negro longshoremen organized the Longshoremen's Protective Union Benevolent Association to cooperate with the existing white local."[240] Apparently, the regular longshoremen, in addition to the screwmen, had also organized by this time and had met with some success. Northrup provides corroboration by noting that in 1865, black and white longshoremen conducted a strike side-by-side.[241] According to Marshall, the 1865 strike was defeated through the use of black strikebreakers.[242] The important point, however, is that organizations of longshoremen were formed in New Orleans before and after the Civil War and included both blacks and whites.

---

236. Marshall, *Labor in the South, op. cit.*, p. 60; and Spero and Harris, *op. cit.*, p. 185.

237. Marshall, *Labor in the South, loc. cit.*; and Herbert R. Northrup, "The New Orleans Longshoremen," *Political Science Quarterly,* Vol. LVII (December 1942), p. 526.

238. *Ibid.*

239. Marshall, *Labor in the South, loc. cit.*

240. Northrup, "The New Orleans Longshoremen," *op cit.*, p. 527.

241. *Ibid.*

242. Marshall, *Labor in the South, op. cit.*, p. 61.

Although racial harmony was often the keynote on New Orleans' docks, a serious recession in 1873 caused whites and blacks to engage in fierce job competition that led to riots and bloodshed.[243] According to Marshall:

> Although white workers, with the aid of the politicians, gradually took over an increasing number of longshoring jobs, they were able to do so only by agreeing to accept the same low wages paid to Negroes. And the Negroes who were barred from these jobs stood ready to undercut wage rates.[244]

The screwmen, although isolated by their skill from the oversupply of labor, felt the need to protect themselves from the competition and, in 1875, established the Screwmen's Benevolent Association, No. 1, for Negroes.[245] In return, the black screwmen agreed to uphold the screwmen's wage rate and to supply no more than 100 screwmen (20 gangs) for work at any one time. This arrangement left the white screwmen in firm control of the bulk of the employment opportunities.

During the 1880's New Orleans longshoremen conducted many strikes and the organization of the port proceeded rapidly.[246] In 1881, labor in New Orleans formed the Central Trades and Labor Assembly which was probably unique to the extent that it encouraged black and white union representatives to affiliate and to work together. In November 1892, this Central Trades Assembly conducted ". . . the first general strike in American history to enlist the skilled and unskilled labor, black and white, and to paralyze the life" of an entire city.[247] This little known strike lasted three days and ended in a compromise settlement

243. See *ibid.*, and Northrup, "The New Orleans Longshoremen," *loc. cit.*

244. Marshall, *Labor in the South, op. cit.*, p. 61.

245. See Northrup, "The New Orleans Longshoremen," *op. cit.*, p. 528; and Carroll George Miller, "A Study of the New Orleans Longshoremen's Unions from 1850 to 1962," unpublished Master's thesis, Louisiana State University, 1962, p. 15.

246. *Ibid.*, p. 16.

247. Roger W. Shugg, "The New Orleans General Strike of 1892," *Louisiana Historical Quarterly*, Vol. XXI (April 1938), p. 347. The fact that this strike occurred in the South, where reunionization had been weak, has caused historians to ignore it, and the further fact that this article was placed in a local journal of limited circulation has maintained that ignorance.

which failed to win the key union demand for closed shop agreements. The waterfront unions did not break their contracts by participating, but the leaders of the screwmen were selected to direct the strike.[248]

Racial harmony again broke down, however, in 1894 when the white screwmen struck the port over alleged violations of the working agreement by both black screwmen and employers. This strike, supported by the general longshoremen, resulted in serious violence and bloodshed directed at working blacks and later at employers who had the benefit of a police department that protected employed Negroes.[249] An employer-sought federal injunction halted the strike and the strikers returned to work under the old 1875 agreement,[250] but the racial solidarity of waterfront workers was broken for the time being.

1900 to 1930: Destruction of Unions

In 1901, sufficient racial harmony had been restored to permit the formation of the Dock and Cotton Council which ". . . included unions of screwmen, general longshoremen, teamsters, yard men, cotton classers, scalehands, and cotton weighers . . . [with] the screwmen dominat[ing] the council. . . ."[251] Also at this time, the New Orleans longshore unions affiliated with the newly formed ILA.[252] A 1901 strike for higher wages saw both black and white longshoremen again striking side-by-side.[253] Racial harmony was promoted further when in 1902, the two screwmen's association agreed to divide the work on a fifty-fifty basis between the races.

A strike in 1907 saw racial harmony at its best, but it also signalled the beginning of the end for longshore unions. The following quotation is illustrative of the racial solidarity existing along the waterfront.

---

248. *Ibid.*, p. 554.

249. Miller, *op. cit.*, pp. 17-19.

250. *Ibid.*, p. 19.

251. Marshall, *Labor in the South, op. cit.*, p. 63.

252. *Ibid.*

253. Northrup, "The New Orleans Longshoremen," *op. cit.*, p. 528.

> [T]he whites and Negroes were never before so strongly cemented in a common bond and in . . . 39 years . . . [there was never] such solidarity. In all the previous strikes the Negro was used against the white men, but that condition is now past and both races are standing together for their common interests.[254]

The strike was called when negotiations over the number of cotton bales to be loaded reached an impasse. The strike grew to include the teamsters and general longshoremen when it was learned that sailors were being used as strikebreakers, but it ended when the mayor pressured the parties into accepting arbitration.[255] Important, however, is that the effects of technology was being felt and the importance of the screwmen was beginning to erode.

Led by the screwmen, the Dock and Cotton Council in 1921 precipitated a strike that resulted in the heavy use of strikebreakers (both black and white) and the use of nonunion labor, on a permanent basis, by some of the largest shippers in the port.[256] Since the cotton press rendered obsolete the screwmen's skill, the companies found ready replacements in the oversupply of Negroes that had been admitted to the black local on an open door policy and who had been sharing, unequally, the available work with the less numerous white longshoremen. A 1923 strike, again led by the screwmen, resulted in all companies turning to nonunion labor, both Negro and white, causing the virtual disappearance of active unionism.[257] Only the piers operated by the United States Shipping Board continued to employ union longshoremen.[258] This open shop employment policy prevailed on the docks for the next decade.

According to Spero and Harris, all four strikes between 1916 and 1923 were controlled by white waterfront workers. The "rabbits", or casuals, picked up to fill extra job openings during peak periods, were used as prime strikebreakers. Most, if

254. As quoted in Arthur Raymond Pearce, "The Rise and Decline of Labor in New Orleans," unpublished Master's thesis, Tulane University, 1939, p. 68.

255. Marshall, *Labor in the South, op. cit.*, p. 64.

256. *Ibid.*, p. 69.

257. Northrup, "The New Orleans Longshoremen," *op. cit.*, pp. 532-533.

258. This ended in 1931 when the shipping board leased its piers to private operators who locked out the remaining union members.

not all, of these men were black except in 1923 when many white strikebreakers were used.[259] It is apparent, therefore, that the militancy of the white longshoremen, coupled with an oversupply of black longshoremen, led to the downfall of New Orleans longshore unions.

1930 to the Present

Many of the white longshoremen who gained entrance to the industry through strikebreaking activities in 1921 and 1923 soon after were eliminated. As part of the open shop policy, the employers placed all hiring in the hands of Alvin E. Harris, a Negro. Harris' identification methods insured that union adherents and most whites would not receive employment.[260] The data in Table 21 indicate that if many whites had gained longshore employment during the 1921 and 1923 strikes, they were not permanent positions. The black participation rate increased by almost 10 percentage points between 1920 and 1930. If the following quotation correctly illustrates that as late as 1926, whites were driving Negroes off New Orleans docks, then Harris' methods were felt after that date:

> In some places in the South, however, due to the sharp struggle for jobs whites are competing so with Negroes for this work that they are actually driving them out of these occupations. This is particularly applicable to New Orleans, where in 1926 it was reported that the Negro dock workers there had been largely superseded by Italians and Latin Americans.[261]

The open shop hiring system under Harris reversed this trend. Spero and Harris noted that the proportion of blacks to whites in 1930 was greater than the approximate 4 to 1 ratio apparent during the 1923 strike.[262] Moreover, the racial harmony which existed during the years before union strength was broken, was based on blacks receiving less than an equal share. Work, as already noted, was divided between black and white locals, but not on the basis of membership. Hence, the individual Negro received less than a fair share. On the ship, blacks were as-

---

259. Spero and Harris, *op. cit.*, pp. 187-190.

260. Northrup, "The New Orleans Longshoremen," *op. cit.*, p. 533.

261. Greene and Woodson, *op. cit.*, p. 308.

262. Spero and Harris, *op. cit.*, p. 186.

TABLE 21. *Longshore Industry*
Total and Negro Employment
Louisiana, 1910-1970

	1910	1920	1930	1940	1950	1960	1970
Total	2,654	4,390	5,322	3,874	4,870	4,722	3,644
Negro	1,588	2,862	3,953	2,719	3,734	3,561	2,499
Percent Negro	59.8	65.2	74.3	70.2	76.7	75.4	68.6

Source: Tables 5, 6, 7, pp. 41, 42, 44.

signed jobs in the hold, and whites worked the deck. Spero and Harris point out that:

As the price of accepting the Negro as a co-worker, the white man declared that the black man would have to work where he did not want to. He created different positions on the vessel for the two races, taking the side of the ship next to the wharf for himself and assigning the side away from the wharf to the Negro. Although this form of Jim Crowism worked no actual hardship, it was an indication of the absence of real labor solidarity.[263]

Although unions continued to exist in the 1923-1933 period, their strength and bargaining power was so small that management was free to ignore them and operate without contracts. The passage of the National Industrial Recovery Act of 1933, in part recognizing and supporting union organization, gave impetus to the employers to create "independent" company unions. In keeping with past practice, the "new" locals were racially segregated and signed contracts with the employers.

In 1934, the ILA attempted to gain control of the "independent" unions by revoking the charters of its old locals and issuing new charters to new groups. Surviving supporters of the old locals took issue with the ILA action, however, and were able to win a court order enjoining the revocation.[264] Nevertheless, independents remained in control of the waterfront.

Indication of the strength of the independents can be seen during a strike of all Gulf Coast ports in 1935 when the volume of work handled in New Orleans increased substantially. Since ILA Locals 231 and 1226 had no control, they were powerless to prevent the company from working.[265]

In 1936, however, the ILA once again revoked the old charters, for alleged improper conduct that was upheld in the courts, and issued new charters to the company unions as General Longshore Workers, ILA Locals 1418 for whites and Local 1419 for blacks.[266] During the 1936-1938 period, the number of whites receiving longshore jobs steadily increased, apparently as a reresult of political pressure to relieve unemployment among

263. *Ibid.*, p. 191.

264. Miller, *op. cit.*, p. 30.

265. *Ibid.*, pp. 31-32.

266. Northrup, *Organized Labor and the Negro, op. cit.*, pp. 150-151.

whites at the expense of the then politically powerless blacks.[267] Some evidence for the above can be noted in Table 21 which shows that white participation rate in the industry increased slightly during the 1930 and 1940 period.

In 1937, the West Coast International Longshoremen's and Warehousemen's Union (ILWU) conducted an organizing campaign in New Orleans preaching equality between the races and gaining the support of those Negroes who were not regularly employed.[268] The Negro leadership, the employers, and the city police, who conducted raids on the alleged Communist ILWU headquarters, and especially regularly working white and black longshoremen, all supported the ILA with the result being an overwhelming ILA victory in a NLRB representation election.[269] The ILA victory was aided by ". . . the expenditure of $63,825.14 for 'direct and indirect' education by the ILA colored local," [270] but also indicated solid support of the ILA by the black longshoremen who worked more regularly.

During the next few years, and after World War II, the white local embarked upon an employment stabilization program whereby the membership would share equally the available work. A restriction on admission to the local became an integral part of the policy. On the other hand, the black local's strength weakened and the employment of its members became unstable. This resulted from a continuing open shop policy, recurring financial difficulties, mismanagement, and defalcations.[271]

According to census data in Table 21, the black participation rate increased during the 1940-1950 period. In large measure this is attributable to Local 1419's open admission policy rather than some exercise of control over the entrance and hiring process. Many men considered themselves longshoremen, although relatively few earned a decent income on the waterfront. The data in Table 22, covering the 1956-1963 period provide convincing evidence of this fact.

---

267. From the field notes of that period of Professor Herbert R. Northrup.

268. Miller, *op. cit.*, p. 35.

269. Marshall, *Labor in the South, op. cit.*, pp. 207-208.

270. Northrup, *Organized Labor in the South, op. cit.*, p. 150.

271. Marshall, *Labor in the South, op. cit.*, p. 209.

As can be seen in Table 22, at least one-half of all those receiving longshore employment during 1956-1963 worked less than 800 hours per year. In 1962-1963, only 7 percent of the longshore work force worked more than 1,600 hours, a figure approaching full-time employment.[272] Over the entire period, the number of men employed ranged between 11,500 and 15,500 annually, although the weekly demand averaged between 6,000 and 6,200.[273] The resultant oversupply of labor perpetuated an extremely casual port.

By 1962, according to Miller, this oversupply of black labor was encouraged both by the black local's open door policy and the drifting away of whites from the docks. At that time, he found that 73 percent of the longshoremen were black and that separate locals existed "mainly as a result of custom rather than discrimination. On the docks both races are hired, associate and work together in integrated groups." [274] According to Miller, economic realities fostered and maintained integration:

> On the docks both races are hired, associate, and work together in integrated gangs. Although many of the employers and the foremen are prejudiced and would prefer to hire only white longshoremen, they must hire some colored because there are not enough white longshoremen available. About 73 per cent of the longshoremen are colored and the hiring foremen, most of whom are white, find it necessary to hire some Negroes at all times. If they do not, the Negroes will refuse to work for them and they will be unable to hire the minimum gang necessary to work during busy periods or in times of labor shortages. Thus, the foremen are forced to hire at least some colored; and the white, if they want to work, must work in the integrated gangs.[275]

Miller also found a trend for white longshoremen to drift away from the docks and for the white local to be unable to recruit replacements.[276] This trend has continued and membership now below the 1,000 mark with many of those older men soon to retire. If present development continues within ten years the

---

272. U.S. Department of Labor, *Manpower Utilization—Job Security in the Longshore Industry, Port of New Orleans, Report and Findings* (Washington: 1964), p. 28.

273. *Ibid.*, pp. 26-27.

274. Miller, *op. cit.*, p. 64.

275. *Ibid.*

276. *Ibid.*, pp. 64-65.

TABLE 22. *Longshore Industry*
Percent Distribution of New Orleans Longshore Work Force by Hours Worked, 1956-1963

Contract Year	Total Longshore Employment	Percent of Employees Working: Less Than 100 Hours	100-799 Hours	800 Hours or More
1956-1957	15,486	39.0	17.1	43.9
1957-1958	10,085	29.6	17.1	53.3
1958-1959	12,198	30.6	18.3	51.1
1959-1960	14,306	39.1	18.8	42.1
1960-1961	12,224	34.6	19.5	45.9
1961-1962	11,668	33.7	18.4	47.9
1962-1963[a]	13,226	44.2	16.2	39.6

Source: U.S. Department of Labor, *Manpower Utilization—Job Security in the Longshore Industry, Port of New Orleans, Report and Findings* (Washington: 1964), p. 27.

[a] 1962-1963 covers New Orleans only, however, other years include New Orleans and Baton Rouge, La., also.

labor force of the New Orleans docks may well be entirely black.[277]

The Situation in the 1970's

Table 23 shows the racial composition and approximate number of longshoremen by union locals. The fact that the locals report substantially more members than the longshore census (see Table 21) may be attributed to census undercounts, faulty union data, and to the fact that many longshoremen may hold other jobs and report their work to census enumerators as other than longshore.

The bulk of longshoremen are found in the general longshore locals. Although the white local, Local 1418, has nearly 1,000 members, less than 800 are active. The others maintain their membership for pension or for other security purposes. As Miller found, attrition without replacement is drying up the white local.

The banana handlers, once a key "craft" are also disappearing. Standard Fruit and Steamship Company has moved its operations to Gulfport, Mississippi, leaving only United Fruit using once busy New Orleans banana wharves. Containers are fast making banana handling by a special group obsolete.

277. Interviews, New Orleans, July 1973.

TABLE 23. *Longshore Industry*
Racial Composition and Jurisdiction of New Orleans International Longshoremen's Association Locals, 1970

Local	Jurisdiction	Approximate Membership	Race	
			Negro	White
1418	General Longshore Workers	1,000		all
1419	General Longshore Workers	4,000	all	
1683	Sack Sewers, Sweepers, Etc.	140 [a]	all	
1802	Sack Sewers, Sweepers, Etc.	145		all
854	Freight Car Handlers	841	821	20 [b]
1497	Clerks and Checkers	475	7	468 [c, d]
1655	Dray Clerks	100	1	99
1515	Banana Handlers	110		all
1800	Banana Handlers	300	all	

Source: Confidential information in the author's possession.

[a] Includes 11 females.

[b] These men always worked freight cars, but prior to 1962 were members of Local 1418.

[c] Plus an additional 125 white and 6 Negro casuals.

[d] See text for comment on number of black clerks and checkers since 1970.

During the labor contracts which ran from 1964 to 1968, agreements were made to decasualize the docks. The white longshoremen (Local 1418) had no problem because of previous limits on membership and attrition, however, as noted previously the blacks (Local 1419) finally reached agreement in 1967. Under the rules now in effect, registered men must be employed for jobs if available; if a nonregistered man is hired when a registered one is available, the company must pay into a fund an amount equal to what it paid the nonregistered man. Top seniority people are guaranteed a stipulated number of hours worked per year; of these, 738 were white and 2,247 were black in July 1973. For the payroll period ending July 16, 1973, blacks worked 78.3 percent of the hours.[278]

Groups are employed in New Orleans through an employer operated hiring hall, the only such type in a major American port. Men have to be able to produce and the gang as a unit has to be productive for the foreman to get the job. Today,

278. Data from New Orleans Steamship Association.

white foremen have mixed gangs—often as few as three whites and ten to fifteen blacks depending on the product moved—whereas black foremen invariably have an all-black gang. Employers claim that it is becoming increasingly more difficult to recruit a white foreman who can "control" black dominated gangs, predicting that the white foreman, as well as the white longshoreman, will disappear from the docks by 1985. As of mid-1973, 133 or 36.8 percent of the foremen were black, as compared with 228, or 63.2 percent, who were white. Ten years earlier, only 20 percent of the foremen were black.[279]

To become a foreman, a man must have experience and a following—he must be able to produce a gang and provide substitutes for absenteeism. Because longshoremen and foremen have separate pension plans, a longshoreman who accepted a promotion prior to 1967, could lose his longshoremen pension rights if he were not already vested. In that year, a reciprocal arrangement between the two pension plans was worked out, and with this obstacle overcome, the number of blacks willing to take on a foreman's job increased substantially. As a result of decasualization, however, the average age of black longshoremen in 1973 was 47. With a substantial member of these illiterate or having very little education, many do not aspire to, or cannot achieve, a supervisory role.

Foremen in the longshore industry in most ports are union members; in New Orleans, they are not required to belong to the union, but many do in order to maintain union rights in case of a possible reduction in employment. Superintendents are not union members and maintain a separate pension plan in New Orleans without reciprocal arrangements with those of foremen or longshoremen. Moreover, with longshoremen paid $5.55 per hour in 1973, and provided numerous fringe benefits, including premium overtime, a man promoted to superintendent may be forced to accept a reduction in pay. Employers attribute this, poor educational background, and past discrimination to the reason why only a few black superintendents have been recruited since 1965.

As in most ports, the clerks and checkers are largely white, but some progress has been made since 1970 when only one black checker was reported. Now ten blacks are in the top checker seniority list of those who work regularly, as compared with 440 whites. The New Orleans Steamship Association refused to go

279. Data from New Orleans Steamship Association.

along with the proposed checker local decasualization plan during the 1964-1968 contract because the local declined to accept the black checkers which the Association insisted must be a part of the arrangement. The local finally agreed during the 1968-1971 contract, and now two of the ten blacks are in supervisory positions and all were given seniority credits for past employment. In addition, approximately one-half of the 200 clerks and checkers with "C" seniority ratings—that is, who are called to work after the top list is exhausted—are also black.

As part of the traditional black-white relationships on the New Orleans waterfront, Negroes did not press for clerks and checkers jobs and whites ceded the freight handing work to blacks.[280] The Civil Rights Act of 1964 made this informal arrangement illegal, and a few whites have been admitted to Local 854, the freight car handlers. Since these jobs are considerably less desirable, whites have not sought to share in them.

Unlike the situation in most other ports, gangs in New Orleans have been integrated since 1937, a year that corresponds to the chartering of the former company unions by the ILA and the beginning of the attempts of the West Coast ILWU to wrest bargaining rights for the port—attempts thwarted by the loyalty of black longshoremen to the ILA. Not until the late 1950's and early 1960's, however, was work within gangs fairly assigned, blacks continued to be relegated to work in the holds and the off-side of ships, etc. The employers now claim all this has ended.

> It used to be that a white man could come out on the docks and get a deck job. Now the hold men would not stand for it. The work depends on productivity and safety. The gang, as a unit, has to be productive to get work. Men have to produce for the foremen to get jobs. If men in the hold feel that they should get the deck job and do not because the foreman picks another man, dissension arises and production goes down. The senior black men coming out of the hold insist that they get the deck jobs. They have to be able to produce and to operate the winches, but if they can, they get the job.[281]

Table 24 shows the number and percentage of blacks used in five preferred jobs in what the New Orleans Steamship Association avered to be nine representative stevedoring companies for four periods between March 1965 and December 1972. In all but one—pilemen, which is disappearing as a function—blacks have a majority of the jobs, in all of them their share has increased, and in

280. Miller, *op. cit.*, p. 65.

281. Interview, employer representative, New Orleans, July 1973.

TABLE 24. *Longshore Industry*
Number and Percent of Regular Gang Members by Race in Deck and Wharf Jobs, New Orleans Nine Representative Companies—Four Periods, 1965, 1970, 1972

	March 1965		March 1970		April 1972		December 1972		Percent Difference
	Number	Percent	Number	Percent	Number	Percent	Number	Percent	1965-1972
Winchmen									
Black	182	69.5	216	80.3	164	83.2	132	82.0	+12.5
White	80	30.5	53	19.7	33	16.8	29	18.0	—12.5
Total	262	100.0	269	100.0	197	100.0	161	100.0	
Derrickmen									
Black	123	93.9	139	98.6	110	97.3	82	95.3	+ 1.4
White	8	6.1	2	1.4	3	2.7	4	4.7	— 1.4
Total	131	100.0	141	100.0	113	100.0	86	100.0	
Hookonmen									
Black	113	43.1	174	64.4	138	69.7	129	72.1	+29.0
White	149	56.9	96	35.6	60	30.7	50	27.9	—29.0
Total	262	100.0	270	100.0	198	100.0	179	100.0	
Drivers									
Black	112	42.7	178	61.4	126	62.1	119	66.1	+23.4
White	150	57.3	112	38.6	77	37.9	61	33.9	—23.4
Total	262	100.0	290	100.0	203	100.0	180	100.0	
Pilemen									
Black	22	24.4	40	41.2	34	54.8	31	47.0	+22.6
White	68	75.6	57	58.8	28	45.2	35	53.0	—22.6
Total	90	100.0	97	100.0	62	100.0	66	100.0	

Source: New Orleans Steamship Association.

three of the five, that share is equal or greater than their overall share of waterfront jobs.

Despite these evidences of racial harmony and improvement, a large number of discrimination cases have been filed with the Equal Employment Opportunity Commission, and several have been consolidated in a court case awaiting hearing before the United States District Court in New Orleans. The complaint alleges that discrimination exists, among other reasons, because:

> ... Negroes are virtually excluded from work as carpenters, clerks, safety men, timekeepers and superintendents. While not entirely excluded from work as lift truck operators and foremen, a disproportionately small number of Negroes are hired to work in these positions.
>
> White employees in all job classifications are assigned more work and work of a less onerous nature than their Negro counterparts.
>
> Negroes are denied equal promotional opportunities to positions such as foreman, superintendent, and other supervisory jobs. . . . [T]he ILA locals are also segregated by race.[282]

In reply to these charges, the industry maintains that these charges are largely based upon situations elsewhere, particularly on the Texas ports, and not New Orleans. Moreover, the racial division of labor, as Miller pointed out a decade ago, exists despite gang integration and does not perpetuate discrimination.

A key to the discrimination case is the charge that blacks earn less than whites because of discrimination. That blacks do, on the average, earn less than whites, is apparently correct because the employers attribute this to high black absenteeism. Thus, the New Orleans Steamship Association provided data to the Industrial Research Unit showing that during the same nine months in 1968, the average earnings for whites was $6,370 and for blacks $5,200 and the average rate of absenteeism for whites was 10.4 percent and 21.4 percent for blacks. The longshoremen with the best attendance record had the highest earnings. Earnings of a gang where compared to gang absenteeism using a rank order correlation and the coefficient of correlation was between 0.96 and 0.99. Whatever the outcome of the litigation, gross earnings of the members of the black Local 1419 often are substantial, as shown by Table 25, which is presented as a typical week in the "busy session", usually six to eight months of the year.

---

282. Summons for *George James Williams* v. *New Orleans Steamship Ass'n*, Civil Action No. 70-873 (D.C. New Orleans, 1971).

TABLE 25. *Longshore Industry*
Percent Distribution of Gross Earnings
Local 1419, New Orleans
Week Ending March 26, 1973

Gross Earnings	Number of Men	Percent of Total
Less than $100	277	12.8
$100-199	599	27.7
$200-249	496	22.9
$250-299	414	19.1
$300-349	195	9.0
$350-399	112	5.2
$400-449	42	1.9
$450-499	15	0.7
$500 and over	16	0.7
Total	2,166	100.0

Source: New Orleans Steamship Association.

New Orleans—Final Comment

In no other port has there been a longer history of black-white cooperative relationships on the waterfront than in New Orleans. This relationship has not always been equitable, and has often been strained. Yet integration progressed earlier and farther than in other ports, North or South. It now appears that the white longshoremen will, within this decade, pass into history regardless of the outcome of current litigation.

MOBILE AND EASTERN GULF PORTS

Neither Mobile to the East, nor the Texas ports to the West, have developed racial employment relationships similar to those in New Orleans, although, as in New Orleans, unionization came early to these ports. Thus, Professor Northrup found that in Mobile "both white and colored longshoremen succeeded in forming local unions in the late nineteenth century, which later affiliated with the ILA." [283] Professor Marshall provides corroboration by noting that the Colored Longshoremen's Benevolent Association was formed in Mobile in 1894 and that in 1914 the white longshoremen of

283. Northrup, *Organized Labor and the Negro, op. cit.*, p. 148.

Mobile quit work in sympathy with Negroes belonging to this group who were striking for higher wages.[284]

Although most authorities claim that a 1923 strike was the catalyst to black control of the Mobile waterfront,[285] census data indicate that blacks comprised a large majority of the work force in the 1910-1920 period (see Table 26). The 1923 strike, which was in sympathy with New Orleans longshoremen, was soundly defeated by the use of nonunion Negro strikebreakers. It is apparent, therefore, that if blacks were not dominant in the Mobile waterfront prior to 1923, they certainly were after that date.

The defeat of the 1923 strike caused the destruction of the ILA in Mobile, as it had in New Orleans, and in Gulfport, Mississippi, as well, where the ILA locals also went out in sympathy with their New Orleans fellow workers.[286] Unlike the situation in Mobile, however, the blacks did not obtain a job monopoly in the ports of Mississippi, Panama City or Pensacola, Florida, where whites and blacks traditionally divided the work.[287]

The 1923-1931 period was marked by the complete absence of ILA activity in Mobile, in Mississippi and in the western Florida ports as well. In 1931, however, the ILA chartered a new local in Mobile, Local 1284, that functioned with little effectiveness until strengthened by the National Industrial Recovery Act. By 1934, the port of Mobile was completely organized and in June 1934, the union called a strike.[288] Employers broke the strike by using white strikebreakers and by forming an independent association.

When unrest continued on the docks, an international ILA representative came to Mobile and engineered a deal whereby the charter of the existing local was revoked and a new charter was granted to the "independent," which immediately signed a closed-shop contract with the employers' association. Dues in the new local were raised to 4 per cent of total earnings. The white strikebreakers were then driven from the docks and again only Negroes were employed.[289]

---

284. Marshall, *Labor in the South, op. cit.*, p. 67.

285. See, for example, Northrup, *Organized Labor and the Negro, op. cit.*, p. 148.

286. Marshall, *Labor in the South, op. cit.*, p. 69.

287. Greene and Woodson, *op. cit.*, p. 308.

288. Marshall, *Labor in the South, op. cit.*, pp. 204-206.

289. Northrup, *Organized Labor and the Negro, loc. cit.*

TABLE 26. *Longshore Industry*
Total and Negro Employment
Alabama, 1910-1970

	1910	1920	1930	1940	1950	1960	1970
Total	888	1,117	1,443	1,272	1,112	1,080	752
Negro	715	1,010	1,383	1,173	1,036	1,027	652
Percent Negro	80.5	90.4	95.8	92.2	93.2	95.1	86.7

Source: Tables 5, 6, 7, pp. 41, 42, 44.

The independents' contract was taken over by the ILA and extended to Gulfport and Pensacola and to Mobile.[290]

These tactics, combined with rumors of graft and corruption led to an attempt by the ILWU, as in New Orleans, to win bargaining rights for the port of Mobile. Fear that a change would instigate black-white competition and that an ILWU victory would result in a port boycott by other workers led to a narrow ILA victory.[291]

Throughout the 1940's, 1950's and the early 1960's, Mobile remained an extremely casual port. According to the U.S. Department of Labor, in 1964 "the present (1964) workforce far exceeds maximum requirements of the port." The Department noted that of 3,380 total employees, 54 percent worked less than 100 hours during the year, 24 percent worked between 100 and 700 hours, 18 percent worked between 700 and 1,600 hours, and only 4 percent worked more than 1,600 hours.[292]

Mobile, like other ILA ports, is now decasualized, however, blacks remain the sole longshore labor force. As in the South Atlantic ports, there are few black checkers or supervisors above the foremen level. Past discrimination and a declining labor force, which is a by-product of decasualization, means that few opportunities for advancement are available.

Table 27, based on Equal Employment Opportunity Commission data for a few establishments, confirmed this black domination of the blue collar jobs and white hegemony for white collar positions. The only exception, however, is that maintenance workers around the port are predominantly white. The situation in other Gulf ports is dissimilar to that in Mobile in several ways. This is shown by the data on ILA local unions—and one independent—in this area that is set forth in Table 28.

Although blacks outnumber whites in the Gulfport, Mississippi, longshore industry, whites do a disproportionately large share of the available work. This stems from an agreement between the races that reserved for whites all work involving a special cargo press, such as banana and other fruit handling, and all general cargo movement was reserved for black longshoremen. Unfortunately for blacks, the agreement was made before some large fruit

---

290. Marshall, *Labor in the South, op. cit.*, p. 205.

291. Northrup, *Organized Labor and the Negro, op. cit.*, pp. 148-149.

292. U.S. Department of Labor, *Manpower Utilization—Job Security in the Longshore Industry, Port of Mobile, Report and Findings* (Washington: 1964), p. 29.

TABLE 27. *Longshore Industry*
Employment by Race and Occupational Group
Mobile, Alabama, SMSA, 1966, 1969, 1970 [a]

Occupational Group	1966			1969			1970		
	Total	Negro	Percent Negro	Total	Negro	Percent Negro	Total	Negro	Percent Negro
Officials and managers	44	—	—	26	—	—	45	—	—
Professionals	1	—	—	1	—	—	1	—	—
Technicians	—	—	—	—	—	—	2	—	—
Sales workers	—	—	—	—	—	—	—	—	—
Office and clerical	70	—	—	74	—	—	76	1	1.3
Total white collar	115	—	—	101	—	—	124	1	0.8
Craftsmen	55	41	74.5	53	28	52.8	32	24	75.0
Operatives	86	52	60.5	114	110	96.5	46	29	63.0
Laborers	1,271	1,226	96.5	455	447	98.2	527	525	99.6
Service workers	—	—	—	1	1	100.0	1	1	100.0
Total blue collar	1,412	1,319	93.4	623	586	94.1	606	579	95.5
Total	1,527	1,319	86.4	724	586	80.9	730	580	79.5

Source: U.S. Equal Employment Opportunity Commission, 1966, 1969, 1970.

[a] Data cover 6 establishments in 1966, 3 establishments in 1969, and 4 establishments in 1970.

TABLE 28. *Longshore Industry*
Union Membership by Race
Selected Gulf Coast Locals
1973

Local	Location	Jurisdiction	Approximate Membership	Race	
				Negro	White
1410	Mobile, Ala.	Maintenance Division	60	4	56
1410	Mobile, Ala.	General Longshore	1,300	1,295	5
1410-1	Mobile, Ala.	Warehouse	80	80	
1459	Mobile, Ala.	Clerk and Checker	80		80
1752	Pascagoula, Miss.	Longshore	150	125	25 [a]
1303	Gulfport, Miss.	Longshore	300	Most	
795	Gulfport, Miss.	Special Cargo	200		Most [b]
1482	Panama City, Fla.	Longshore	Unk.		Unk. [c]

Source: Personal investigation.

[a] All 25 are probably clerks and checkers, since by custom, clerks and checkers belong to 1752.

[b] These men perform a disproportionately large share of work, since the amount of special cargo moving in and out of Gulfport has increased over the years.

[c] This local is *not* part of ILA. A racial strike led to secession and exclusion of blacks.

companies moved their operations from New Orleans to Gulfport. As a result, the amount of special cargo moving through Gulfport has increased dramatically over the years, at the same time the amount of general cargo has remained small, as it has in most minor ports.

The situation in Panama City, Florida, is unique to Gulf Coast ports. The ILA local in the city conducted a strike several years ago which led to the secession of the local from the ILA. The strike was over racial matters and the newly created independent union which excluded blacks from membership. This resulting white dominance over general longshore work is not duplicated anywhere else along the Gulf Coast.

The segregated locals in Pensacola, Florida, are facing charges similar to those filed in Baltimore, Maryland, and in the Texas ports. At present, the EEOC is investigating charges of referral discrimination and unequal work distribution. Pending the outcome, government will seek to have the locals merge their membership rolls, seniority systems, and hiring halls. It will be interesting to note the results because in Baltimore, the courts ruled in favor of local union and seniority merger, but left separate gangs as the only vestige of segregation although in Texas, the courts ruled against merging the locals, but did merge the hiring halls and the seniority structures. The Texas cases are explored in depth is the next section.

THE TEXAS PORTS

The ports of Texas, especially Galveston and Houston, have grown in importance over the years both in terms of the amount of cargo handled and in the job opportunities available to black longshoremen. This section will develop the role of Negroes and longshore unions in Texas concentrating on Galveston, and to a lesser extent on Houston, since they are the primary Texas ports.

In both these primary ports, activity can be related to the overall economy of the cities. For example, port activity is important to the overall economy of Galveston.

> The Port of Galveston generated $103.6 million in gross wages and salaries from primary and secondary employment in 1968. This figure represented more than 61 per cent of the total wages and salaries earned in the City of Galveston during that year. . . . No other single segment of the economy was as significant to the City of Galveston as the Port in terms of income.[293]

In only 50 years, the Port of Houston has developed, as a result of the construction of its ship channel, from an insignificant river town to become one of the largest and busiest ports in the nation. The data on cargo movements presented in Table 2 (p. 9) indicate that between 1950 and 1970, the Port of Houston ranked near the top of all major ports in the United States. It is readily apparent that port activity, especially port generated employment, has a profound impact upon Houston's total economic climate.

Early Unionism: The Galveston Screwmen

The rise of cotton as the chief commodity in the Texas economy spurred the development of organization among the cotton screwmen. Unlike the New Orleans screwmen, the Galveston Screwmen's Benevolent Association (SBA), at the time of its formation

293. Warren Rose, "The Port of Galveston: Employment and Income Impact," mimeographed report prepared for Galveston Wharves, 1970, p. 47.

in 1866, was composed of foremen and stevedores already near the top of their profession and more interested in mutual benefit matters, such as sickness and death benefits, than in matters of wages and hours.[294] Although the SBA adopted the constitution prepared by the New Orleans screwmen, it did not adopt the New Orleans objectives. Instead it chose to restrict membership and to control job opportunities by preventing the employment of sailors and Negroes.[295] The membership of SBA was ". . . one-third German, one-third Irish, and one-third native white."[296]

Soon after its formation, however, the SBA began admitting regular screwmen, resulting in a more economic set of objectives. Important, however, is that

> [t]he Association [continued to prevent] Negroes from entering the occupation and thereby eliminated a potential competitive threat to its position. By 1875, a closed shop hiring arrangement was imposed on stevedores employing members of the union. Certainly this organizational power is unparalleled in the early Texas labor movement.[297]

Taylor notes that the strength of the SBA was so great that black screwmen posed no real threat until after 1880.[298] The SBA monopoly power was maintained despite the fact that in 1870, black longshoremen formed the Longshoremen's Benevolent Association and in 1876 a Negro Screwman's Benevolent Association was also formed.[299] In fact, both the SBA and the Longshoremen's Benevolent Union, the white forerunner of the Longshoremen's Benevolent Association, forbade their respective members from working with Negro dockworkers prior to the formation of black unions.[300]

An increased demand for labor made the Negro's entrance to cotton screwing possible. By 1878, white screwmen were not able to furnish

294. Allen Clayton Taylor, "A History of the Screwmen's Benevolent Association from 1866 to 1924," unpublished Master's thesis, University of Texas, 1968, pp. 45-46.

295. *Ibid.*, p. 68.

296. Marshall, *Labor in the South, op. cit.*, p. 65.

297. Taylor, *op. cit.*, p. 45.

298. *Ibid.*, p. 72.

299. Lawrence D. Rice, *The Negro in Texas, 1874-1900* (Baton Rouge: Louisiana State University Press, 1971), p. 189.

300. These were constitutional restrictions applied in 1869. See Taylor, *op. cit.*, p. 72; and Rice, *op. cit.*, p. 189.

the requirements of the season's peak. In addition, the white man's refusal to load more than seventy-five bales without overtime pay facilitated the Negro's entrance.[301]

The increased demand led to the formation, in 1879, of the all-black Cotton Jammers' Association (CJA). This union, along with the Longshoremen's Benevolent Association, (LBA), ". . . made inroads into the white-dominated work and as a result tended to increase the racial antagonism of all concerned." [302]

As the amount of cotton moving through Galveston increased in the 1882-1900 period, so too did the competition between blacks and the SBA. In 1883, the CJA was able to obtain work on the Galveston waterfront by underbidding white screwmen, thus, doing so precipitated a strike in which the SBA gained no concessions from employers.[303] Adding to existing racial difficulties was that in 1884, the CJA and LBA were admitted to the Galveston Trades Assembly.[304] In the following year, the Knights of Labor conducted a sympathetic strike in Galveston against the Mallory Line, and the employer responded by replacing the strikers with Negroes.[305]

The irony is that the striking Knights of Labor may have been black longshoremen. According to Taylor, in 1891 the SBA made a large purchase of new tools and equipment in order to meet the growing competition from a group known as "Screwmen's No. 2." Taylor notes that this group may have been the remnants of the Knights of Labor "Screwmen's Assembly No. 4583." [306] Since the literature notes that the SBA competed with only groups of black longshoremen, it may have been that the Knights of Labor in Galveston was all-black and that the Mallory Line used Negro strikebreakers against Negro strikers.

In an attempt to maintain job control, the SBA, in 1891, along with the purchase of new tools, reduced the gang size in order to supply all the gangs demanded by employers. This was another

---

301. Taylor, *op. cit.*, pp. 84-85.

302. Rice, *op. cit.*, p. 189.

303. *Ibid.*

304. *Ibid.*

305. *Ibid.*, pp. 189-190.

306. Taylor, *op. cit.*, p. 97.

attempt to prevent the employment of black screwmen who, nevertheless, continued to find work.[307]

By 1898, approximately 2,300 black longshoremen had affiliated with the Colored Labor Protective Union.[308] In that year, the organization conducted a strike against Mallory demanding an increase in wages. The company responded as it had on previous occasions; this time promising to use whites, at higher than the prevailing wage, as well as Negro strikebreakers.[309] During the strike, which involved riots and bloodshed, the Colored Labor Protective Union was granted an AFL charter as Federal Labor Union No. 7147.[310] The strike, however, was defeated as the company imported blacks from Houston and other areas to act as strikebreakers.[311]

During the same year, the ILA chartered an all-black longshore group in Sabine Pass, Texas, as ILA Local 51. A strike and subsequent wage settlement caused dissatisfied whites, who had later affiliated with Local 51, to quit and to move to Port Arthur, Texas,[312] which hastened the demise of the local.

1900 to 1930

As it had in New Orleans, the early 1900's marked the beginning of the end for the Galveston screwmen as an elite and powerful union. Faster ships, with bigger holds, made time spent in port screwing cotton less profitable; the high density cotton press was introduced to Galveston, and the SBA was facing increased competition from black screwmen. Along with the CJA, the white screwmen were competing with the Lone Star Cotton Jammer's Association (LSCJA), another all-black screwmen's group formed in 1901.[313] The LSCJA secured employment by working for wages lower than those paid to both SBA and CJA members.

307. *Ibid.*, p. 96.

308. Rice, *op. cit.*, p. 190.

309. *Ibid.*

310. *Ibid.*, p. 191.

311. *Ibid.*

312. *Ibid.*

313. Taylor, *op. cit.*, p. 113.

At the turn of the century, Galveston had approximately 2,500 to 3,000 longshoremen who were either nonunion or belonged to independent unions.[314] ILA activity, which began in earnest at this time, coupled with increased competition among SBA, CJA, and LSCJA members led Pearce to comment that ". . . in Galveston a condition of slavery exists because the races are at variance."[315] As might be expected, violence and bloodshed accompanied ILA activity.[316]

ILA efforts continued, however, and were successful. The white longshoremen in Galveston were the first to be organized, receiving an ILA charter in 1900 as Local 310.[317] The SBA was organized as Local 307 in 1902 after opposition from Local 310 was surmounted.[318] The CJA was organized as Local 329 in 1911 and the LSCJA became Local 851 in 1913.[319] Mention is not made in the available literature concerning the date black longshoremen were organized, giving rise to the assumption that by the first decade of the twentieth century all the screwmen's groups were performing regular longshore work and that the distinctions between screwmen and longshoremen had become inoperative.

One year after the CJA became ILA Local 329, the SBA and CJA negotiated a work-sharing agreement whereby the two groups would remain separate entities, but would share equally all available work and both would demand the same pay rates.[320] The employers' refusal to accept the coalition's demands, however, forced both groups to accept the old standards and caused the SBA to abandon the Negro a short time thereafter.[321] The ILA revoked the SBA's charter over this action, but restored it when the SBA promised not to take any work performed by CJA members before the agreement was reached.[322] No further action was taken by the

314. Russell, *op. cit.*, p. 71.

315. Pearce, *op. cit.*, p. 68.

316. Russell, *op. cit.*, pp. 71-72.

317. Taylor, *op. cit.*, pp. 110-111.

318. *Ibid.*, p. 111.

319. *Ibid.*, p. 116.

320. *Ibid.*

321. *Ibid.*, pp. 117-118.

322. *Ibid.*, pp. 118-119.

ILA, giving evidence of the fact that Negro longshoremen were not being treated as first class citizens or union members. The data in Table 29 show that the number of black longshoremen in Texas during this period was substantial and that blacks were becoming a majority of the waterfront work force. By 1920, Negroes represented 57.0 percent of the Texas longshoremen.

In Houston, the ILA was active before the port was opened for deep sea vessels, having organized a black local in 1912 (872) and then later a white local (1273).[323] According to Professor Northrup, the black local ". . . not only permitted the organization of a white local, but signed a ninety-nine year contract for an even division of work between the two locals."[324] Russell notes that

> [ILA Local 1273] dates back to 1914 when Houston was an unimportant but promising port. Work was divided evenly with Local 872—a method still known as the 50-50 system. The men worked in mixed gangs without segregation and there were practically no problems between the races even though the situation had a built-in economic rivalry.[325]

Russell goes on to note that in the 1920's a disturbing situation created by the Ku Klux Klan led to the segregation of Houston's longshore work force.[326]

In 1914, a strike at Port Arthur, Texas, was broken by black strikebreakers. The lost strike resulted in a charter for a Negro local and a fifty-fifty work-sharing agreement.[327]

Most of the current ILA structure in Galveston was created in 1924 when the ILA merged Locals 307 (SBA) and 310 (general longshoremen) into 307. The ILA kept intact Local 329 (CJA) and Local 851 (LSCJA).[328] All of these groups were performing general longshore work.

One of the most significant features of the early Texas longshore industry was that unlike anywhere else, the unions and the employers developed a system of work rotation that produced the first "decasualized" ports in the nation. In most of the Texas ports,

---

323. See Northrup, *Organized Labor and the Negro, op. cit.,* p. 151; and Russell, *op. cit.,* p. 288.

324. Northrup, *Organized Labor and the Negro, loc. cit.*

325. Russell, *loc. cit.*

326. *Ibid.*

327. *The Longshoreman,* Vol. V (August 1914).

328. Taylor, *op. cit.,* p. 127.

TABLE 29. *Longshore Industry*
Total and Negro Employment
Texas, 1910-1970

	1910	1920	1930	1940	1950	1960	1970
Total	2,386	3,601	3,926	4,393	4,044	4,615	4,112
Negro	843	2,052	2,739	2,790	2,142	2,517	1,867
Percent Negro	35.3	57.0	69.8	63.5	53.0	54.5	45.4

Source: Tables 5, 6, 7, pp. 41, 42, 44.

the unions controlled hiring and saw fit to rotate the gangs assigned to work to insure that the work was spread evenly among all members. The work rotation system grew out of the attempts to divide the work between blacks and whites and was made easier by each local maintaining its membership within certain limits. This can be contrasted to other areas, especially New Orleans and most of the South Atlantic ports, where union membership among black longshoremen went unchecked and resulted in a high degree of dissatisfaction among longshoremen, poor earnings records, and the continuation of extremely casual employment practices.

1930 to the Present

The data in Table 29 indicate that blacks increased their share of longshore work in Texas in 1930 and maintained a majority through 1960. Although the ILA remained strong in Texas through the 1920's, having disappeared in other Gulf ports, a strike was lost in 1931 by the use of strikebreakers (presumably black) and wages were cut by 10 cents per hour.[329] In the same year, company unions were established in Beaumont, Port Arthur, and Houston which were eventually eliminated in 1934 after a twelve-day strike.[330]

In 1935, in an attempt to recover its lost strength throughout the Gulf area, the ILA conducted a coastwide strike. The results in other Gulf areas have been cited previously, but, according to Professor Marshall:

> The strike was more effective in the Texas ports, but even some Texas companies reopened with strikebreakers, many of whom were lodged in warehouses. In Houston, Negro and white longshoremen organized independent unions and signed a contract with the Houston Maritime Committee, which divided work equally among Negro and white longshoremen. The employers at Beaumont offered to settle with the ILA, but the union refused because it wanted a Gulf-wide agreement.[331]

The independent unions did not achieve much success nor did they have a long existence, since the ILA remained the dominant union force along the Texas waterfront.

The equal division of work, begun during the early days of organization, continued through the 1930's, through the days of

329. Marshall, *Labor in the South, op. cit.*, p. 203.

330. Herbert R. Northrup, "Negro Labor and Union Policies in the South," unpublished Ph.D. dissertation, Harvard University, 1942, p. 177.

331. Marshall, *Labor in the South, op. cit.*, p. 205.

World War II and even through the late 1960's. Although the system appears to be fair and equitable, it has always operated to reduce the average annual earnings of black longshoremen, and at the same time distribute more work to white longshoremen. This is attributable to the uneven membership rolls of black and white locals, sharing in the available work. Traditionally, black locals have had more members than white locals, therefore, forced to apportion their share of the work among more people.

There is one exception to the fifty-fifty principle in Texas that operated to reduce further the amount of work available to blacks.[332] When port facilities were being built in Brownsville, Texas, in 1934, black longshoremen were refused an ILA charter because there was no corresponding white group in the port. In an effort to win a charter, the black workers aided white longshoremen in organizing to such an extent that the blacks lent whites the necessary initiation fees. Their efforts were rewarded as blacks received a charter as Local 1368 and whites became Local 1367. The employers, however, preferred white longshoremen, resulting in the revocation of Local 1368's charter, until such time as the demand for black longshoremen increased.

Beginning in 1946, the amount of cargo moving through Brownsville increased substantially, thereby prompting the 1948 ILA convention to consider the charter request made by Local 1368. The convention's response was to conduct a two-year investigation which culminated in a 75 to 25 division of work in favor of the white local. The ILA stipulated that the 75 to 25 division must be written into all contracts agreed to by both locals. In addition, the 1950 solution was accompanied by an agreement whereby a black gang from Local 1368 and a white gang from Local 1367 would not be assigned to work side-by-side out of the same hatch. Allegedly, this arrangement was to avoid any turmoil that might ensue. Both locals reluctantly accepted the decision, although Local 1367 was placed in temporary trusteeship when it claimed that more than 75 percent of the work should be under its jurisdiction.

In 1962 and 1963, Local 1368 attempted unsuccessfully to renegotiate the work division formula. The 1963 attempt was

332. The information that follows concerning Brownsville, Texas, is taken from, *International Longshoremen's Association Local 1367*, 148 N.L.R.B. 897 (1964) (trial examiner's decision).

in the form of unfair labor practices charges filed with the National Labor Relations Board. The trial examiner, and later the Board itself, upheld Local 1368 by noting that enforcement of the above arrangements did, in fact, constitute unfair labor practices. The Board issued a cease and desist order restraining employers and the unions from enforcing the discriminatory provisions, but gave no formula for changing the employment practices. That nothing resulted from this order is indicated by the fact that Locals 1367 and 1368 were subsequently named as co-defendants, along with 35 other Texas locals, in a government suit aimed at removing discriminatory union practices in the Texas longshore industry.

In a 1965-1966 NLRB case, the Houston Maritime Association, its member companies, and ILA Local 1351, Clerks and Checkers, were found by the NLRB to have committed violations of the Taft-Hartley Act by refusing to refer blacks for clerk and checker positions.[333] Beginning in 1963, it was found that Local 1351 refused to accept into membership, and refer to job assignments, Negroes who made themselves available as clerks and checkers. In addition, Local 1351 refused to establish a separate local for black clerks and checkers. Instead, the local closed its membership rolls and refused to admit any new members.

The NLRB concluded that the membership freeze acted to perpetuate past acts of discrimination and that Local 1351 did not act to represent fairly all those it was empowered to represent. The trial examiner noted that Local 1351 continued to bar black workers although since 1959 it did not discriminate against white nonmembers.[334]

In the present case, the Board ordered Local 1351 to admit to membership Negro applicants, according to practices in force prior to September 1964. In addition, the defendants were to reimburse all charging parties for loss of earnings and seniority resulting from the above practices. Finally, the defendants were

333. See generally *Houston Maritime Ass'n, ILA Local 1351*, 168 N.L.R.B. 615 (1967) (trial examiner's decision and decision by the Board), *enforcement denied*, 426 F.2d 584 (5th Cir. 1970).

334. The change in policy toward white nonmembers was the result of a suit brought in 1954 and completed in 1964. See *Galveston Maritime Ass'n, Inc.*, 122 N.L.R.B. 352 (1954), *enforced in part, Local 1351, Steamship Clerks and Checkers* v. *NLRB*, 329 F.2d 259 (D.C. Cir.), *cert. denied*, 377 U.S. 993 (1964).

ordered to cease and desist from enforcing any arrangements whereby job referrals were to be based on race or union membership.

An appeal to the Fifth Circuit Court for enforcement of this order was not sustained. In a two to one decision, the court held that acts of racial discrimination had not occurred within the period allowed by law for filing unfair labor practice charges[335] The court found that the closing of the registration books was not a racially motivated act, but was necessitated by legitimate concerns.[336] In summary, the court refused to enforce the Board's order, leaving intact the employment practices enforced since 1964. It must be emphasized here, however, that the foregoing NLRB cases are based on findings of violations of national labor laws and not civil rights legislation. The wide-reaching case, *United States* v. *International Longshoremen's Ass'n,* is based on the 1964 Civil Rights Act and, as will be seen, rests on different principles and concepts of discrimination.

The dual structure of the ILA in Texas is clearly shown by the data in Table 30. In almost every case, a black deep-sea longshore local has a sister white deep-sea longshore local in the same city. The same is true for coastwise and warehouse locals. The major exception, of course, is the clerks and checkers local in Houston. It is clear that this structure represents the most obvious case of union organization based on racial segregation ever to exist in the longshore industry. At the same time, however, the structure has allowed for the development of black locals with their own identities, strong and influential black union leaders, and an economically strong group of black longshoremen. It may well be that if the ILA had organized the Texas ports along nonsegregated lines, blacks would not be in as good an economic position as they are at present.

The current position of black longshoremen, however, is not one of complete equality with whites. The data in Tables 31 and 32 show that there are very few blacks serving in white collar positions in the Texas longshore industry. Although few in number, all white collar positions, including clerks and checkers, have been reserved for whites. In addition, Tables 31 and 32 show that only in recent years, 1969 and 1970, have blacks

---

335. 426 F.2d 584 (5th Cir. 1970).

336. *Ibid.*

TABLE 30. *Longshore Industry*
Approximate Membership by Race
Texas International Longshoremen's Association Locals

Local	Location	Jurisdiction	Approximate Membership	Race	
				Negro	White
1351	Houston	Clerk and Checker	n.a.		X
872	Houston	Deep Sea	1,100	X	
1273	Houston	Deep Sea	1,005		X
1231	Houston	Coastwise	Merged with 1273[a]		X
1271	Houston	Coastwise	Merged with 872[a]	X	
1330	Houston	Warehouse	180		X
1331	Houston	Warehouse	175	X	
1525	Houston	Warehouse	200	X	
1581	Houston	Warehouse	150	Mexican-American	
440	Port Arthur	Deep Sea and Warehouse	60	X	
1029	Port Arthur	Deep Sea	64		X
1175	Port Arthur	Deep Sea	105	X	
325	Beaumont	Deep Sea	77	X	
1306	Beaumont	Deep Sea	75	X	
1610	Beaumont	Deep Sea	96		X
341	Orange	Deep Sea	20		X
814	Orange	Deep Sea	42	X	
1723	Freeport	Deep Sea	20		X
1818	Freeport	Deep Sea	50	X	
307	Galveston	Deep Sea	200		X
329	Galveston	Deep Sea	180	X	
851	Galveston	Deep Sea	400	X	
1576	Galveston	Deep Sea	140	Mexican-American	
1367	Brownsville	Deep Sea	48		X
1368	Brownsville	Deep Sea	45	X	
1372	Brownsville	Coastwise	n.a.		X
636	Texas City	Deep Sea	n.a.		X
991	Texas City	Deep Sea	n.a.	X	
1405	Texas City	Warehouse	n.a.		X
1406	Texas City	Warehouse	n.a.	X	
1224	Corpus Christi	Deep Sea	73		X
1225	Corpus Christi	Deep Sea	75	X	

TABLE 30. *Continued*

Local	Location	Jurisdiction	Approximate Membership	Race	
				Negro	White
1241	Corpus Christi	Coastwise	Merged with 1225[b]	X	
1245	Corpus Christi	Coastwise	Merged with 1224[b]		X
1280	Corpus Christi	Warehouse	15		X
1281	Corpus Christi	Warehouse	16	X	
1758	Port Lavaca	Deep Sea	18	X	
1763	Port Lavaca	Deep Sea	25		X

Source: Pre-trial brief for Plaintiff, *United States* v. *International Longshoremen's Ass'n,* Civil Action No. 69-B-3 (S.D. Tex. 1970), Appendix pp. 2-30. Post-trial brief for Plaintiff, *United States* v. *International Longshoremen's Ass'n,* Civil Action No. 69-B-3 (S.D. Tex. 1970), Appendix pp. 15-32.

[a] Prior to merger in late 1968, Local 1271 had 86 blacks and Local 1231 had 60 whites.

[b] Date of merger and approximate membership unknown.

maintained a majority of the blue collar positions. Even among blue collar occupations, blacks did not comprise a majority of the "craftsmen" occupations in any of the years covered by Tables 31 and 32. The percentage of black craftsmen fell from 46.5 percent of total in 1966 to 37.0 percent in 1970—barely one-third of all craftsmen positions in the Texas industry (see Table 31). It is clear, therefore, that although blacks outnumber whites in terms of union membership, whites seem to be closer to the top of the job hierarchy. In addition, the fifty-fifty work division agreements maintained by all longshore locals in Texas into 1972 operated to allot only one-half of all available work to black longshoremen who comprised more than one-half of the total longshore work force.

The above arguments formed the basis of a government civil rights suit aimed at securing a merger, and, therefore, a more equitable distribution of work among black and white locals performing the same job in the same geographical area. In its complaint, the government alleged that the ILA, the ILA South Atlantic and Gulf Coast districts, and the 37 ILA locals ". . . are engaging in a pattern and practice of discrimination against

TABLE 31. *Longshore Industry*
Employment by Race and Occupational Group
Texas, 1966, 1969, 1970 [a]

Occupational Group	1966			1969			1970		
	Total	Negro	Percent Negro	Total	Negro	Percent Negro	Total	Negro	Percent Negro
Officials and managers	59	—	—	58	—	—	54	1	1.9
Professionals	5	—	—	4	—	—	132	—	—
Technicians	—	—	—	3	1	33.3	1	1	100.0
Sales workers	4	—	—	6	—	—	2	—	—
Office and clerical	112	—	—	97	—	—	92	1	1.1
Total white collar	180	—	—	168	1	0.6	281	3	1.1
Craftsmen	170	79	46.5	137	59	43.1	376	139	37.0
Operatives	8	4	50.0	499	261	52.3	1,140	772	67.7
Laborers	3,700	1,270	34.3	1,108	516	46.6	431	140	32.5
Service workers	1	—	—	—	—	—	—	—	—
Total blue collar	3,879	1,353	34.9	1,744	836	47.9	1,947	1,051	54.0
Total	4,059	1,353	33.3	1,912	837	43.8	2,228	1,054	47.3

Source: U.S. Equal Employment Opportunity Commission, 1966, 1969, 1970.

[a] Data cover 11 establishments in 1966, 11 establishments in 1969, and 9 establishments in 1970.

TABLE 32. *Longshore Industry*
Employment by Race and Occupational Group
Houston, Texas, SMSA, 1966, 1969, 1970 [a]

Occupational Group	1966			1969			1970		
	Total	Negro	Percent Negro	Total	Negro	Percent Negro	Total	Negro	Percent Negro
Officials and managers	21	—	—	24	—	—	22	—	—
Professionals	2	—	—	1	—	—	1	—	—
Technicians	—	—	—	—	—	—	—	—	—
Sales workers	2	—	—	4	—	—	2	—	—
Office and clerical	67	—	—	64	—	—	63	—	—
Total white collar	92	—	—	93	—	—	88	—	—
Craftsmen	—	—	—	4	1	25.0	158	76	48.1
Operatives	6	4	66.7	497	261	52.5	480	264	55.0
Laborers	2,500	569	22.8	487	236	48.5	87	47	54.0
Service workers	1	—	—	—	—	—	—	—	—
Total blue collar	2,507	573	22.9	988	498	50.4	725	387	53.4
Total	2,599	573	22.0	1,081	498	46.1	813	387	47.6

Source: U.S. Equal Employment Opportunity Commission, 1966, 1969, 1970.

[a] Data cover 4 establishments in 1966, 6 establishments in 1969, and 3 establishments in 1970.

persons on account of their race in the operation of their labor organizations in the State of Texas." [337] The patterns and practices were made operable by the maintenance of (1) separate union locals based upon race; (2) the division or apportioning of work based upon race; and (3) the assignment of persons to work in specific job areas based upon race.[338] The government alleged that the above does not allow for ". . . the full enjoyment by all persons of their rights to equal employment opportunities." [339]

More specifically, the government charged that ". . . the maintenance of racially segregated locals, chartered on the basis of race, is a *per se* violation of Title VII of the Civil Rights Act of 1964; and that, in any event, the maintenance of such segregated locals tends to and does in fact deny to Negro longshoremen employment opportunities which are equal to those of similarly experienced and qualified white longshoremen." [340] The above allegation is predicated upon the fact that ". . . the work in each port (except Brownsville) is assigned on a segregated basis, each race supposed to receive 50 per cent of the work, although Negro longshoremen account for approximately 65 per cent of the total number of longshoremen. . . ." [341] The above assignment included gangs assigned to different ends of the same ship and the assignment of walking bosses or supervisors.

In depositions taken prior to the trial, ILA officials, including President Gleason, testified that all ILA locals ". . . chartered prior to 1963 [were] chartered because of the race of the respective members." [342] In addition, it was admitted that each local can be identified as either white or black.[343]

The United States government requested that the locals be ordered to merge in all areas where separate black and white

337. Complaint for Plaintiff p. 8, *United States* v. *International Longshoremen's Ass'n*, Civil Action No. 69-B-3 (S.D. Tex. 1970).

338. *Ibid.*

339. *Ibid.*

340. Pre-trial brief for Plaintiff p. 3, *United States* v. *International Longshoremen's Ass'n*, Civil Action No. 69-B-3 (S.C. Tex. 1970).

341. *Ibid.*

342. *Ibid.*, p. 6.

343. *Ibid.*

groups were performing the same work. In addition, the government asked that seniority lines be merged with each member of a new local maintaining the seniority he had in his old local. The government asked also for merging of hiring halls, observance of strict seniority in filling out gang requirements, and a merging of assets.

In defense of their practices, the locals cited as defendants presented *no* briefs or gave no defense at the trial. In testimony at the trial:

> Negro union officials . . . urged the Court not to order a merger. They say that by the maintenance of "sister locals" in every port, the Negroes, by having their own unions and their own union officials, have been able to better themselves by being able to hold high positions in their locals, and have been recognized in the community as a separate, powerful voice for the Negro communities, and has attained for them and the Negro people of the community, a standing which they could not have otherwise attained.[344]

Basically, the union contended that black longshoremen would be harmed rather than helped if the government was granted the requested relief.

The district court ruling can be summed up in the following statement.

> The basic finding that the Court is making in this cause is that the Defendants have chartered and still maintain locals on a segregated basis, that the prevalent rule of dividing the work fifty-fifty between the White and Negro locals violates Title VII of the Civil Rights Act of 1964, because it deprives longshoremen, be they Black or White, Anglo, Mexican-American or Negro, equal working opportunities depending on which group is in the majority in the different ports, and that this will be a continuing violation in the future.[345]

The court, however, refused to grant a merging of the locals, feeling that the rights of those who have worked on the waterfront might be jeopardized if welfare plans, pension funds, unequal property holdings, and nonuniversal seniority structures were medged. The court noted that the inequities found to exist could be eradicated without ordering a complete merger.

In line with its findings, the court ordered the parties to meet and draft an agreement acceptable to all and in keeping with

---

344. *United States* v. *International Longshoremen's Ass'n*, 334 F. Supp. 976 (S.D. Tex. 1971).

345. *Ibid.*

the court's conclusions.[346] The court did not, at this time, enter an order or decree. The parties did meet, but could not settle their differences.

In the fall of 1972, the government petitioned the court to enter an order. At a hearing held in May 1973, the court gave the unions three months to develop an acceptable plan or, failing that, the court would enter an order granting *all* requested relief.[347] It is important to note here that since no order has been entered, no appeal has been made.

The decision of the Court in the Texas case is in sharp contrast to the ruling handed down in Baltimore. Although the same form of union organization and racial segregation and discrimination existed in both Baltimore and the Texas ports, the Baltimore locals were ordered to merge, leaving only the segregated gangs as remnants of past practices. In Texas, the court took cognizance of the identity and strength of separate black locals and sought to retain them. It may be that the potential of white dominance, and a concomitant reduction in influence and employment opportunity for blacks, which could result from the Baltimore decision, has been avoided in the Texas case.

It is also possible that if the locals in Texas continue to block the elimination of discriminatory practices, the Court may have no choice but to impose a merger upon them. The judge in the Texas district court noted that he was convinced that Congress did not intend for black union locals to lose their identity and strength when it passed the 1964 Civil Rights Act. The actions of the Texas locals, including the black groups, make it appear as if they are at odds with the court's interpretation.

THE WEST COAST

Although the ports on the West Coast do not have a history comparable in length to those in the East or in the South, the West Coast longshore industry has grown in importance over the years and currently occupies a position of major significance in the industry. The history of unionism on the West Coast is unlike that in the remainder of the industry and the role of blacks in West Coast longshoring does not follow the model

346. Interview, June 1973.

347. *Ibid.*

developed elsewhere. As will be noted below, blacks were introduced into the industry long after unionization had occurred.

The Early Industry: 1850 to 1933

The earliest appearance of economic activity among West Coast longshoremen was a strike that occurred in 1851.[348] Unfortunately, records can not be found concerning any union organization surrounding the work stoppage, but most probably the strike occurred in San Francisco. In 1853, however, the Riggers' and Stevedores' Union Association was formed.[349] This Association was guild-like in orientation, excluding regular longshoremen from membership, and remained a powerful and influential group for many years. It is also likely that the organization developed in San Francisco and it is more than likely that it included no blacks whatsoever.

As the industry grew on the West Coast, so did the group of unskilled, regular longshoremen. In the mid-1880's, two factions of regular longshoremen formed unions. The first was the Longshore Lumberman's Protective Association and the second was the Steamship Stevedore's Protective Union,[350] which affiliated with the Knights of Labor in 1887.[351] A depression in the 1890's, however, caused unionism to ebb only to be revived again in 1898 when the West Coast groups affiliated with the ILA.[352]

In Seattle, Washington, the first attempt at organization was a cooperative operated by the Stevedores, Longshoremen, and Riggers' Union of Seattle in 1889.[353] This was an organization in which the carefully controlled membership owned stock in the cooperative for which they received preferential treatment in hiring.[354] In 1902, approximately 300 longshoremen formed

348. Betty V. H. Schneider and Abraham Siegel, *Industrial Relations in the Pacific Coast Longshore Industry* (Berkeley: Institute of Industrial Relations, University of California, 1956), p. 2.

349. *Ibid.*, p. 4.

350. *Ibid.*

351. *Ibid.*

352. *Ibid.*, p. 5.

353. Larrowe, *op. cit.*, p. 87.

354. *Ibid.*, p. 88.

the Longshoremen's Mutual Benefit Association and affiliated with the ILA; however, one year later, for reasons which are unclear, the Association's charter was revoked.[355] As a result, Seattle longshoremen switched their allegiance to a rival group—Local 1, Pacific Coast Federation of Longshoremen—but financial difficulties in 1904 brought the men back to a weak but operating ILA.[356]

A strike in San Francisco in 1901 was of significance in that it marked the introduction of blacks into the West Coast longshore industry.[357] The use of Negroes as strikebreakers in part aided the employers in breaking the strike and represents the recorded use of blacks anywhere in the industry on the West Coast. The strike was led by the City Front Federation which was formed in 1901. According to Knight, "[f]or the first time in a Bay Area industrial conflict, employers imported large numbers of Negroes from the Middle West." [358] Knight also noted that these men were housed and fed aboard ships anchored away from the docks in order to prevent clashes between the strikers and the strikebreakers. As part of the strike settlement, the employers agreed to retain few, if any, of the strikebreaking black workers.[359]

In 1909, dockworkers formed the Longshoremen's Union of the Pacific. Although it was formed in Portland, Oregon, its was composed of representatives from all Pacific ports.[360] In Seattle, prior to the formation of this group, a strengthened ILA induced employers to establish their own Waterfront Employers Union. As a result, the employers were able to drive out the ILA in 1907-1908.[361]

It is highly doubtful that blacks played a major role in any union organizations during this time period because there were

---

355. *Ibid.*

356. *Ibid.*

357. Northrup, *Organized Labor and the Negro, op. cit.*, p. 152.

358. Robert Edward Lee Knight, *Industrial Relations in the San Francisco Bay Area, 1900-1918* (Berkeley: University of California Press, 1960), p. 79.

359. *Ibid.*, p. 88.

360. Schneider and Siegel, *op. cit.*, p. 6.

361. Larrowe, *op. cit.*, p. 89.

very few, if any, working in the industry. The data in Table 33 confirm this conclusion by noting that in California, in 1910, blacks represented only 1.5 percent of the total work force. Given that Oregon and Washington numbered fewer blacks among the population than did California, it is almost certain that blacks were nonexistent in Northwest longshoring in the 1910-1920 period. William Pilcher notes that as far back as 1922, the Portland, Oregon Waterfront Employers Union had an expressed policy of employing white labor only and that blacks were not even used as strikebreakers.[362]

The 1910-1930 years were characterized by rising and falling fortunes of labor organizations accompanied by several lost strikes. In 1916, the Longshoremen's Union of the Pacific conducted an unsuccessful coastwide strike that was broken, at least in San Francisco, with the aid of Negro strikebreakers.[363] In Seattle, the lost strike resulted in the formation of employer owned and operated hiring halls.[364] In 1919, the ILA had gained sufficient strength in the Northwest and was, therefore, able to win contracts covering all ports in Oregon and Washington. An ill-timed strike in 1920, resulting from a post-World War I decrease in port activity and the desire for job rotation and employment security, was defeated and ended effective unionism in the northwest states for the next thirteen years.[365] In San Francisco during the same time period, the Riggers' and Stevedores' Union was destroyed and IWW-led untimely strikes saw control of the hiring process pass into the hands of the bosses.[366]

In Seattle, the employers were not totally ignorant of the desires of the longshoremen and as a result, embarked upon the nation's first serious attempt at decasualization. The effect of the plan was to remove the "floaters"—those who did not have permanent attachment to the industry—and guarantee that the

---

362. William W. Pilcher, *The Portland Longshoremen* (New York: Holt, Rinehart and Winston, 1972), p. 68.

363. See Northrup, *Organized Labor and the Negro, op. cit.,* p. 152; and Schneider and Siegel, *loc. cit.*

364. Larrowe, *op. cit.,* p. 89.

365. *Ibid.,* p. 91.

366. Schneider and Siegel, *op. cit.,* p. 7.

TABLE 33. *Longshore Industry*
Total and Negro Employment
California, 1910-1970

	1910	1920	1930	1940	1950	1960	1970
Total	2,593	3,728	6,346	6,865	8,481	7,869	6,276
Negro	38	44	91	83	2,032	1,820	1,636
Percent Negro	1.5	1.2	1.4	1.2	24.0	23.1	26.1

Source: Tables 5, 6, 7, pp. 41, 42, 44.

regular longshoremen would receive most of the work on a rotating basis.[367]

In summary, the strikes in 1901, 1916, 1919, and 1920 were all settled in favor of the employers who made partial use of Negro strikebreakers. Prior to their use in these strikes, Negroes "were not welcomed in west coast longshore locals. . . ." [368] As a result of losing these strikes, the bargaining power of West Coast longshoremen was substantially reduced and employers functioned with an open shop until the mid-1930's. Although Negroes made substantial gains as a result of their use as strikebreakers in 1919, most of the advances were lost by 1934.[369]

During the 1922-1934 period, ". . . no union was recognized by the employers; although independent unions continued to exist, they had no voice in determining wages or working conditions on the docks." [370] The census data in Table 33 indicate that the use of Negro strikebreakers did not result in any permanent increase of black longshoremen on West Coast docks. As can be seen, between 1910 and 1940, the black proportion of total longshoremen in California did not exceed 1.4 percent. As noted earlier the black percentage in Oregon and Washington was likely to be lower than in California.

1934 to 1960: Harry Bridges and the ILWU

As it had in other ports, the National Industrial Recovery Act of 1933 spurred the resurgence of active unionism along the West Coast waterfront. A major strike in 1934, involving the complete shutdown of the San Francisco waterfront among other places, marked the strengthening of longshore unionism and the rise to power of Harry Bridges, who first appeared as an official within the ILA and then as the leader of the secessionist International Longshoremen's and Warehousemen's Union (ILWU). The lengthy strike of 1934 represented a major victory for unionism because labor gained control of the hiring hall and, thereby, the hiring process. In Portland, and other

367. Larrowe, *op. cit.*, p. 92.

368. Northrup, *Organized Labor and the Negro, op. cit.*, p. 152.

369. Northrup reports that as late as 1934, there were only 23 Negro ILA members along the West Coast. See, *ibid.*, pp. 152-153.

370. Paul T. Hartman, *Collective Bargaining and Productivity* (Berkeley: University of California Press, 1969), p. 16.

ports, the ILA was able to gain an effective closed shop arrangement.[371] Important, however, is that again Negro strikebreakers were used, especially in San Francisco,[372] and that Bridges was well aware of the need to free the union from the potential damages that could result if the practice were to continue. According to Northrup, "[i]mmediately after the 1934 strike, Harry Bridges, leader of the west coast longshoremen, announced that 'Negro labor will never again find the doors of the San Francisco' longshore locals closed." [373]

Within three years of the 1934 strike, the CIO was formed, another longshore strike occurred on the West Coast, and the West Coast longshoremen seceded from the ILA-AFL to become the ILWU-CIO. Only four locals, all in the Northwest, chose to remain in the ILA. In terms of Negro employment opportunities, however, it appears as though the antidiscriminatory policy of Bridges and the newly formed ILWU brought only minimal change. The data in Table 33 show that in 1940, the black percentage of the California longshore work force stood at the same low figure it had been since 1910. Other census data show that in the same year, Negroes accounted for only 1.1 percent of total longshore employment in the major ports of Seattle, Portland, San Francisco, and Los Angeles, combined.[374]

The reasons for the paradox lie at the very core of ILWU philosophy. One of the causes of ILWU secession from the AFL was the desire of West Coast longshoremen for industrial rather than strict trade unionism. In other words, the dockworkers felt that the occupational differentiations that often accompany craft unionism worked against their best interests. In addition, the desire for local autonomy within a larger national federation was strong among West Coast longshore locals. Under the new ILWU structure, the locals practiced these beliefs. The results included exclusion of black workers. In Portland:

> Long before [World War II] Local 8 [ILWU] had an anti-Negro reputation. During the 1930's, when workers were stirring toward unionization all over the country, Negro dockmen from Gulf ports of the Deep

---

371. Pilcher, *op. cit.*, p. 49.

372. Northrup, *Organized Labor and the Negro, op. cit.*, p. 153.

373. *Ibid.*

374. *U.S. Census of Population: 1940*, Vol. III, *The Labor Force*, Parts 2, 4, 5, State Volumes, Table 13.

South had come out to West Coast ports to seek temporary work among the longshoremen there, to study their militant union tactics for use back home. Those who visited Portland were given a cold shoulder by Local 8 and soon left. The Portland Negro community was miniscule at that time and the incident evoked no local protest, but the "snubbing of brother unionists" infuriated Bridges and other dock leaders from San Francisco.[375]

As will be noted later, the desire of Local 8 to remain free of black labor was so strong that the first Negroes were not admitted until the mid-1960's. It is apparent, however, that local custom and autonomy within the ILWU allowed the Portland local to dictate its own racial policies in opposition to those expressed by the ILWU leadership.

Local 13, in the Los Angeles/Long Beach section of California has a history similar to Portland's Local 8. For example, in the early World War II years of 1940-1942 when approximately 80 longshoremen were added to the area work force coming under Local 13 jurisdiction, only three blacks were included. At the height of the war labor shortage, 1943-1945, 107 blacks were included among the 300 men added to the waterfront. In the postwar years of 1946-1950 only four blacks were among the 80 new men allowed to enter the industry.[376] In fact, the next substantial addition of blacks to the work force coming under Local 13 jurisdiction did not occur until 1963. It is apparent, therefore, that the early history of Local 13, characterized by racial exclusion was relaxed only under conditions of severe manpower shortages.

The above account of the activities of Locals 8 and 13 raises a serious question concerning union democracy and the power and influence of national union leaders. The ILWU was founded, partly, on the desire of West Coast longshoremen for one large industrial union and on the desire for local autonomy within the union structure. The concept of a democratic union in an industrial setting, *i.e.* one that espouses a policy of fair and equal representation for all those who work or seek work in an industry, however, runs counter to the actual occurrences on the West Coast. Although the longshore locals did choose industrial unionism, they preserved discriminatory practices, in

375. Jane Cassels Record, "Race, Jobs, and Unions: The Case of the Portland Longshoremen," address before the Northwest Scientific Association, April 1967, p. 13n.

376. Data developed by personal investigation.

the guise of local autonomy, and were successful in defying the wishes and policies of the national leadership. In fact, at the fourth annual convention of the ILWU in 1941, the delegates adopted a "no discrimination due to race, creed, or color" clause for inclusion in the national constitution.[377] The clause was the culmination of Bridges' efforts to rid his union of racial discrimination, but the results were less than dramatic in port areas that already had ingrained work rules and membership practices that excluded blacks. In essence, some locals within the ILWU might have been practicing democratic principles only for those they allowed memberships utilizing an "exclusion" practice common to most craft unions. The national leadership was ineffective in dealing with the discrimination.

During World War II, some blacks did obtain work permits for the ports in Oregon, but these were rescinded soon after the war.[378] A few years later, the number of Negro casuals in Oregon dwindled to a scarce few.[379] Census data for 1950 indicate that there was one black employed on the Portland, Oregon, docks.[380] As noted above, blacks found work in the Los Angeles/Long Beach area during 1943-1945, but as soon as the war labor shortage ended, blacks again found that work on the docks was being reserved for whites. Yet by 1950, the black percentage of the longshore work force in California had undergone tremendous changes (see Table 33). The reason was Bridges' success in his own city of San Francisco and in Oakland. In 1950, blacks comprised 33.8 percent of the longshore work force in these two areas.[381] Larrowe provides corroboration of the change, and of the paradox faced by Bridges, by noting that

> . . . in San Francisco, largely due to Bridges' efforts during World War II and afterward, a majority of the longshoremen were Black. It was true, nevertheless, that despite the policy of the national union, reaffirmed in convention resolutions time after time since its founding, as recently as the sixties there were ports on the Coast where for days you could watch ships being loaded without once seeing a black longshoreman. In

---

377. *New York Times*, April 9, 1941, p. 28.

378. Confidential memorandum in the author's possession.

379. *Ibid.*

380. *U.S. Census of Population: 1950*, Vol. II, *Characteristics of the Population*, Part 2, State Volume, Table 77.

381. *Ibid.*

some . . . you might believe the explanation that the port was all-white because there weren't any Blacks in the community. But in others—Portland and Los Angeles, for example—the lily-white labor force was obviously the product of a policy of exclusion.[382]

Larrowe, Bridges' biographer and ardent admirer, gives Bridges full credit for the large percentage of blacks in the San Francisco local. A more sophisticated analysis would note that he does indeed deserve credit for his policies, but assign the major cause to the tight post-World War II labor market and the greater availability of work elsewhere for whites. Moreover, although some changes did occur for the better in other West Coast ports between 1950 and 1960, discriminating practices remained. Thus, an unpublished government report relating to Portland states that ". . . the [local] Chapter of NAACP and the Urban League of Portland, Oregon periodically denounced the discriminatory practices of Local 8, as far back as 1956.[383] One source noted that appeals to Harry Bridges, concerning the situation, brought the comment that it was painful, but local autonomy prevented any meaningful international interference or intervention.[384] In Los Angeles/Long Beach in 1958, a warehousemen's local (26) was given a promise that since it was closing its hiring hall, all men, of whom 80 percent were black, would be taken into Local 13. In fact, all but three whites, all Mexican-Americans, and only seven blacks were admitted to membership. Most black warehousemen ended up as casuals working out of Local 13's hiring hall, although many of them had full membership rights in Local 26.[385] Local 13 invoked a sponsorship rule—an existing member must sponsor a new member—to effectively bar the admission of black members of Local 26.[386]

The 1960's

A number of key changes occurred in black participation in the West Coast longshore labor force during the 1960's and particularly in the latter half of that decade. Since these changes varied from port to port, each major port is discussed separately.

382. Charles P. Larrowe, *Harry Bridges: The Rise and Fall of Radical Labor in the United States* (New York: Lawrence Hill and Co., 1972), pp. 366-367.

383. Unpublished memorandum in the author's possession.

384. *Ibid.*

385. *Ibid.*

386. This rule has since been eliminated.

Seattle

As noted in Table 34, the total longshore labor force in Seattle remained stable between 1967 and 1970, but the black work force was reduced by approximately 50 percent between 1969 and 1970. On an occupational basis, blacks were well represented in only the laborer category and even there, the percentage fell from 51.2 percent in 1969 to 10.8 percent in 1970. The black percentage in the other categories reflect the same situations that were found to exist in most of the other regions in the country. There are very few black clerks and checkers in Seattle and relatively few supervisors or foremen (craftsmen) and equipment operators (operatives). The ILWU has four locals in Seattle, but unfortunately membership data for the locals by race are unavailable.

Portland

It was noted earlier that employment opportunities in the Portland longshore industry were refused to blacks since, at least, the early 1920's. It was also noted that only during the severe manpower shortage created by World War II did blacks find waterfront employment, laboring under temporary work permits that were rescinded immediately after the war. The data in Table 35 confirm the fact that through 1971, very little had changed on the Portland waterfront. In a 1961-1964 study prepared by the Oregon Bureau of Labor, it was found that

> . . . Local 8 of ILWU, Portland, Oregon, did have an unwritten policy and system that kept Negroes from being employed as longshoremen on the Portland, Oregon waterfront. It was established at this time that Local 8 of Portland, Oregon was the only ILWU union on the West Coast who openly made it known that they did not want Negro longshoremen.[387]

The longshore work force in Portland is classified into three main groups: "A" men, "B" men, and casuals. In 1961, there were approximately 1,050 "A" men and 150 "B" men working in Portland—none were black—and of the approximately 300 casuals, only 11 were black. There were no other blacks working on any nearby Oregon or Washington docks.[388] It is important to note that only "A" men are union members; "B" men can be offered membership, but in most cases they do not belong to the union.

---

387. Unpublished memorandum in the author's possession.

388. Unpublished memorandum in the author's possession.

TABLE 34. *Longshore Industry*
Employment by Race and Occupational Group
Seattle, Washington, SMSA, 1967, 1968, 1969, 1970

	1967			1968		
Occupational Group	Total	Negro	Percent Negro	Total	Negro	Percent Negro
Office and clerical	220	3	1.4	219	4	1.8
Craftsmen	144	11	7.6	143	13	9.1
Operatives	635	36	5.7	648	35	5.4
Laborers	682	272	39.9	662	270	40.8
Total	1,681	322	19.2	1,672	322	19.3

	1969			1970		
Occupational Group	Total	Negro	Percent Negro	Total	Negro	Percent Negro
Office and clerical	246	6	2.4	240	5	2.1
Craftsmen	169	19	11.2	229	13	5.7
Operatives	647	39	6.0	375	49	13.1
Laborers	557	285	51.2	679	73	10.8
Total	1,619	349	21.6	1,523	140	9.2

Source: Data in author's possession.

Note: By special arrangements with EEOC, the Pacific Maritime Association reports longshore employment data under the above four categories. In general the categories include: office and clerical, clerks and checkers; craftsmen, bosses and highly skilled men; operatives, lower skilled longshoremen and those receiving skill pay differentials; laborers, the bulk of the regular longshoremen.

TABLE 35. *Longshore Industry*
Employment by Race and Occupational Group
Portland, Oregon, SMSA, 1966-1971

Occupational Group	1966 Total	1966 Negro	1966 Percent Negro	1968 Total	1968 Negro	1968 Percent Negro	1969 Total	1969 Negro	1969 Percent Negro
Office and clerical	157	—	—	245	—	—	338	—	—
Craftsmen	231	—	—	235	9	3.8	235	9	3.8
Operatives	545	—	—	477	18	3.8	470	18	3.8
Laborers	858	71	8.3	377	14	3.7	385[a]	19	4.9
Total	1,791	71	4.0	1,334	41	3.1	1,428	46	3.2

Occupational Group	1970 Total	1970 Negro	1970 Percent Negro	1971 Total	1971 Negro	1971 Percent Negro
Office and clerical	309	—	—	212	7	3.3
Craftsmen	237	9	3.8	226	—	—
Operatives	349	18	5.2	421	6	1.4
Laborers	500	19	3.8	432	25	5.8
Total	1,395	46	3.3	1,291	38	2.9

Source: Data in author's possession.

Note: See Table 34 for occupational definitions.

[a] Includes small number of service workers.

In 1963, as part of a coastwise expansion of the longshore work force, the registration books for "B" longshoremen in Portland were opened. Local 8 made national headlines by agreeing to allow blacks to be registered among the new "B" men, thereby putting them in line for future membership.[389] The result of this effort was that 46 blacks became the first of their race ever to be registered for longshore work in the State of Oregon. The issue of union membership, however, raised the same question as was stated earlier—these men were not guaranteed the security of employment attached to union membership. At the time the registration plans were being formulated, Harry Bridges was quoted as saying, "The first thing is to get them to work. . . . Later they can talk about getting in the union." [390] Bridges went on to note that there were no assurances that they will be offered immediate membership and that "[e]ach local is autonomous and decides on its own members. . . ." [391]

The "movement upward" for blacks continued in 1967 when Local 8 inducted 55 new men into the "A" list; among them were 3 blacks.[392] Undoubtedly, these men were given union membership. In the same year, Local 40, clerks and checkers, admitted 9 blacks among the 225 men added to their "B" list.[393] The obvious conclusion to be drawn from the new registrations and from the data in Table 35 is that progress in Portland has been extremely slow in coming and that black representation in the longshore work force remains at a token level ten years after the passage of the 1964 Civil Rights Act in an industry that has offered extensive employment opportunities to blacks in other parts of the country.

San Francisco

The obvious bright spot for black employment in the West Coast longshore industry is San Francisco. The data in Table 36 show that Negroes comprise a sizable proportion of all job classifications, except for office and clerical, throughout the 1967-1971 time period. These data became even more significant when it is noted that the

---

389. See *New York Times*, August 10, 1963 and September 11, 1963.

390. *New York Times*, August 10, 1973.

391. *Ibid.*

392. Unpublished memorandum in the author's possession.

393. *Ibid.*

TABLE 36. *Longshore Industry*
Employment by Race and Occupational Group
San Francisco, California, SMSA, 1967-1970

Occupational Group	1967			1968		
	Total	Negro	Percent Negro	Total	Negro	Percent Negro
Office and clerical	791	24	3.0	833	29	3.5
Craftsmen	441	168	38.1	427	171	40.0
Operatives	1,478	703	47.6	1,516	746	49.2
Laborers [a]	2,490	1,469	59.0	2,322	1,499	64.6
Total	5,200	2,364	45.5	5,098	2,455	48.2

Occupational Group	1969			1970		
	Total	Negro	Percent Negro	Total	Negro	Percent Negro
Office and clerical	791	40	5.1	892	114	12.8
Craftsmen	564	200	35.5	491	210	42.8
Operatives	1,475	811	55.0	1,108	596	53.8
Laborers [a]	2,292	1,451	63.3	1,955	877	44.9
Total	5,122	2,502	48.8	4,446	1,797	40.4

Source: Data in author's possession.

Note: See Table 34 for occupational definitions.

[a] Includes a small number of service workers.

black percentage of the total population in San Francisco is approximately 12 percent and in Oakland it increases to approximately 20 percent. It is apparent, therefore, that the egalitarian principles set down by Bridges soon after the 1934 strike have been applied in a very meaningful way in San Francisco. Equally apparent, however, is that most of the improvement in black employment exhibited in the census data contained in Table 33 can be attributed to San Francisco alone and that little, if any, was done elsewhere on the West Coast to carry out the equal employment policies of the ILWU.

Considering San Francisco alone, however, there is every reason to expect that the racial composition of the longshore work force will follow the trends exhibited elsewhere in the country. On the East Coast and in the South and Gulf Coast regions, more and more of the waterfront work has gravitated to black workers. The same is obviously true in San Francisco.

Los Angeles/Long Beach

It was noted earlier that Local 13, the dominant longshore local in the Los Angeles/Long Beach port area, has a history of black exclusion. It was also noted that one of the vehicles used to perpetuate the exclusionist practice was the "right of sponsorship" requirement maintained by the union. With a 99 percent white membership, it is not difficult to see that the sponsorship rule could be effective. The data in Table 37, however, indicate that considerable change has occurred in the 1967-1971 period. As can be seen, the black percentages in the operative and laborer classifications indicate that Local 13 must have admitted many more blacks than ever before. It is almost certain that the Negroes in the operative category are union members since they are "A" status longshoremen and it is probable that some of the laborers, *i.e.* "B" status longshoremen, also are union members.

Encouraging also is the number of blacks in the office and clerical category—clerks and checkers. Although the actual number is still quite low, the increase from 4 to 23 between 1967 and 1971, does represent a step in the right direction. The same is true for the craftsmen category, a group composed of walking bosses, gang bosses, foremen, and heavy equipment operators. Again, although the absolute number of blacks serving in these capacities is low, the increase from none in 1967 to 21 in 1971 is most encouraging.

TABLE 37. *Longshore Industry*
Employment by Race and Occupational Group
Los Angeles/Long Beach, California, SMSA, 1967-1971

Occupational Group	1967 Total	1967 Negro	1967 Percent Negro	1968 Total	1968 Negro	1968 Percent Negro	1969 Total	1969 Negro	1969 Percent Negro
Office and clerical	497	4	0.8	445	4	0.9	496	11	2.2
Craftsmen	551	—	—	448	—	—	609	17	2.8
Operatives	1,198	294	24.5	1,385	339	24.5	1,657	439	26.5
Laborers[a]	2,152	505	23.5	1,458	332	22.8	1,176	236	20.1
Total	4,398	803	18.3	3,736	675	18.1	3,938	703	17.9

Occupational Group	1970 Total	1970 Negro	1970 Percent Negro	1971 Total	1971 Negro	1971 Percent Negro
Office and clerical	560	24	4.3	559	23	4.1
Craftsmen	490	6	1.2	510	21	4.1
Operatives	1,561	409	26.2	1,328	204	15.4
Laborers[a]	1,525	270	17.7	1,529	168	11.0
Total	4,136	709	17.1	3,926	416	10.6

Source: Data in author's possession.

Note: See Table 34 for occupational definitions.

[a] Includes a small number of service workers.

It is unfortunate that some locals on the West Coast were able to inhibit severely the growth of job opportunities for blacks in the industry and that the national union was, in fact, powerless to combat them. But it is also significant that in other areas, blacks have made solid advances and the recalcitrant locals have begun to make meaningful changes.

CHAPTER IV

Concluding Observations

The longshore segment of the water transportation industry represents a microcosm of the economic laws of supply and demand. The manpower requirements of the employers change daily as does the pool of manpower able to meet the demand. The industry is unique because each port constitutes a separate entity with customs and characteristics that differentiate one from another. Although there are a few large firms in the industry, not one firm truly dominates employment practices and technological innovations. Instead, there are employer associations designed to present a common front in negotiating with a powerful union structure. In this sense, longshore has much in common with such industries as construction and urban transit.

The racial practices and policies are unique also in that in some ports, blacks have always been in the majority and in others, blacks were not welcomed. Yet in others, blacks and whites have shared the available work. The following paragraphs outline some of the major determinants of industry racial policies and their impact upon black employment.

DEMAND FOR LABOR

Black workers have been significant in the industry since the first hogsheads of tobacco were loaded on the wharves of Virginia's ports. Moreover, as the demand for labor has increased, so has the number and proportion of blacks in most ports. In areas where blacks were traditionally excluded, such as in certain West Coast ports, and certain aspects of the work in South Atlantic, Gulf, and eastern ports, breakthroughs have usually occurred in times of shortages of labor. In recent years, the tendency has been for the longshore work force to become increasingly black in nearly all points. The reason, of course, has been the greater ease of whites to obtain work elsewhere, particularly in periods of tight labor markets which have been featured most of the last decade.

THE NATURE OF WORK

For most of its history, the longshore industry has been a model of the casual industry which has been characterized by large fluctuations in the daily demand for labor. Despite recent improvement in job security through decasualization, there remains much uncertainty over the duration of current employment and the probability of future work opportunities. As such, it is not surprising to find that the industry has become unattractive to many whites who have alternate opportunities in industries that afford greater security. Considering the fact that blacks are less well educated and suffer greater restrictions on employment mobility and alternatives, it is not surprising then to note that the longshore industry has become more dependent upon blacks to meet its daily manpower requirements. It is quite clear that the characterization intermittency of employment and the arduous nature of the work itself are the prime reasons behind the historically high demand for blacks in longshoring.

On the supply side, the generally high wage rates offered by the industry proved attractive to blacks who, in many cases, could not find employment elsewhere. The high wage rates, however, were often deceiving because frequent periods of unemployment led to lower than expected total earnings. In essence, the wage rates led to greater supply; greater supply led to less work per man; and less work per man led to lower total earnings. The employers favored this structure, since it guaranteed that suitable labor would always be available to meet the peak demand periods.

The positions of foremen, gang boss, clerk, and checker constitute the upper end of the job spectrum in the longshore industry. In these occupations the ports across the country do not differ. Historically, the major portion of these positions have been filled by whites in every port. This is in contrast to the uniqueness of the regular longshoremen in each port. The reason is quite simple; these jobs are better paying, require less physical exertion, and carry much prestige and influence among the total waterfront labor force. In addition to these few jobs, however, there are few skilled occupations that attract labor which would prefer such work to other opportunities.

THE TIME AND NATURE OF THE INDUSTRY'S DEVELOPMENT

Throughout the Racial Policies of American Industry series, it has been hypothesized that the beginnings of an industry may well determine how its policies become institutionalized, what is required to change them, and under what circumstances they will, in fact, be changed. The longshore industry provides a good example of this. The fact that the longshore industry is an ancient one, as old as ships that sailed the seas, led to the use of slave labor in the South at an early stage and the custom of using blacks in this work. As aspects of the work became more desirable, or as others won control of the jobs in other ports, they too became an institutionalized factor in the work force. Thus, wave after wave of immigrants in New York City developed a section of the work which "belonged" to them. The only way that Negroes could break into this circle was through strikebreaking. When the unions further institutionalized custom, it took the full force of the federal government, plus declining interest in whites, to alter the racial composition of certain areas in recent years.

THE MORES OF THE COMMUNITY

In certain areas, longshore work has been considered only fit for blacks. In other areas, it is considered key work for various ethnic groups. The wide variation of community mores in various parts of the United States is reflected in the character of the longshore force over the years. Now, more and more, the type of work done by longshoremen is considered "low-class work" despite the high remuneration. Under these circumstances one can predict that longshore work will continue to become more and more a black man's job.

CONSUMER MARKET ORIENTATION AND CONCERN WITH IMAGE

Some companies and industries analyzed in our Racial Policies of American Industry series have had their racial policies profoundly affected by their concern that the sales of the products which they market will not be hurt by any racial problems or difficulties. And others have moved in the racial policies area because of the concern with the company or chief executive's image in the community. The longshore industry produces a service that it sells to other companies. And the companies involved are largely small and unconcerned with their image in the community. These factors, therefore, do not appear to have any effect whatsoever in determining company or industry racial policies in the longshore industry.

THE IMPACT OF TECHNOLOGY

Technology has not been a strong factor in the longshore industry but it has had an impact upon its racial policies. The development of the automatic cotton press eliminated a stronghold of white unionism in the South—the screwman's unions. The rise of the container has transferred work from New York to New Jersey and the Port of Newark and thereby benefited blacks. The elimination of the passenger ship by the jet air line has largely impacted on white longshoremen rather than black. Although, as we learned in our study of the offshore maritime industry, the impact on the offshore personnel was heavily felt by blacks. Insofar as mechanization has reduced overall employment, it has impacted apparently proportionately on whites and blacks. Overall, however, our findings in this study, which are quite different from most, have been that the impact of technology has been proportionately beneficial to blacks rather than harmful.

LOCATIONAL FACTORS

Locational factors have been favorable to black employment in longshore work in two ways. First, the ports are urban centers and nearly all such centers had, and still do have, a concentration of black population which places them near the source of work. In addition variables account for a large portion of the increase. These variables include: (1) the growth in importance of Gulf Coast and West Coast longshoring; and (2) a concomitant decrease in the importance of the New York side of the Port of New York.

Changes in the concentration of longshore employment over the years have favored the South Central and the West Coast regions. It has been shown that the size of the longshore work force in these regions has grown relative to the remainder of the industry. In the Gulf Coast region, this has meant that more opportunities have become available to blacks since the union locals there have a tradition of a fifty-fifty work division between the races. Although whites do a greater proportion of the work than blacks and since blacks outnumber whites, the absolute amount of work going to blacks has been increasing and, therefore, black employment has been increasing.

In New York, it has been shown that although the New York side of the port has experienced decreases in the volume of cargo moving through the waterfront, the New Jersey side has been expanding. For black longshoremen, this has meant an increase in work opportunities, since the Elizabeth and Newark areas are worked by a heavily black group in contrast to Brooklyn and Manhattan. Seniority arrangements in the area prevent longshoremen on the predominantly white, New York side from securing employment preferences on the New Jersey side.

The tremendous growth in West Coast longshoring has also created job opportunities for blacks, although some ports in the region have been most resistant to integration. The port of San Francisco, by far the most important in the area, has experienced a very large increase in black employment stemming, for the most part, from labor market factors, but also assisted by the policies of the ILWU.

UNION STRUCTURE AND INFLUENCE

The union structure in the longshore industry favored an oversupply of labor. This was especially true with the black locals of segregated union organizations in the South, but also true in New York City.

Union organization has existed in the longshore industry for as long as there has been an identifiable industry itself. As has been shown, union organization perpetuated the ethnic composition of the longshore work force, perpetuated racial divisions within the work force, created and preserved work assignments based upon real or artificial skill differentials, and was probably instrumental in inducing the formation of employer associations among shippers and stevedores when it became evident that individually, employers were at a disadvantage. Union organization has also operated to retard technological improvement, and this has affected job distribution, and probably the number of jobs available.

Contrary to the practices in most other industries, unionism has served to advance the status of key black longshoremen in many ports and has created influential and powerful black union leaders. Most important, however, is that except for a few isolated instances, blacks have been organized along with whites since unionism was first advanced in the industry. In several key cases, blacks were used as strikebreakers forcing the union establishment to recognize that blacks were a potential threat to union and employment security and that blacks should be allowed to enter the industry and the union.

The ILA has always followed an open admissions policy. The reason is that more members means more monthly dues and, therefore, greater financial security for the union. This policy, of course, was one reason why the ILA vigorously opposed decasualization attempts that would reduce the size of the longshore work force. Resulting directly from this policy, however, was an oversupply of labor, reduced employment opportunities and total earnings for members, and graft and corruption surrounding available job opportunities.

This policy impacted heavily upon blacks in southern longshoring as the black locals placed no restrictions upon membership. On the other hand, the white locals in New Orleans and the Texas ports did limit membership with the result that whites received a proportionately greater share of the work than blacks because the longshore work was divided on a fifty-fifty basis between white and black locals and the black locals had a larger membership.

On the West Coast, the ILWU has always taken a strong stance against discrimination, but its national leaders, like those of the ILA, have been hesitant to challenge the discriminatory practices of locals. As a result, blacks were discriminated against by ILWU locals in Long Beach, California, and Portland, Oregon, until the mid-1960's.

GOVERNMENT POLICIES

It has only been recently that the government has attempted to exert its influence in the longshore industry with the expressed aim of achieving a more equitable division of work among competing black and white locals and hopefully to achieve a merger of these organizations. Whether there will be any long-run benefits accruing to black longshoremen as a result of these efforts can not be answered at this time. Certainly, the potential for both "help and harm" is present. In Baltimore, the accomplished merger of black and white locals could serve to decrease the power and influence of black union leaders or it could increase that power. In turn, this may lead to a decrease in job opportunities available to blacks in the port despite the fact that they represent a majority of the longshore work force or it might expand those opportunities.

On the other hand, in Houston and the other Texas ports, the government may be successful in accomplishing a redistribution of available work that could only serve to strengthen the position of blacks there. If the work is divided on the basis of the number of available workers, blacks will gain a greater share of the work than the fifty-fifty division between union locals currently affords them. It is interesting to note that the leaders of the black locals in the Texas ports have been resistant to the proposed changes. They fear they will lose some of the power and influence which they have maintained in both their communities and unions if the present structure is altered.

Equally interesting is that in both the Baltimore and Texas cases, the clerks and checkers locals were not included in the litigation. According to government sources, this is attributable to governmental ignorance concerning the importance of the clerks and checkers and the amount of discrimination practices by these locals.[394] It is more likely that the government did not include the clerks and checkers because whites would then agitate for a greater share of certain warehouse and regular longshore jobs that have been reserved for blacks. It is interesting to note, in the light of this failure of the federal government to act, that the New York state equal employment agency successfully opened the ranks of the checkers' local in the Port of New York by extended litigation several years before the federal government acted.

FINAL COMMENTS

A currently popular theory of the economics of discrimination finds less than full support in this study.[395] It has been advanced that those firms or industries with long histories of black employment, or with histories of slow growth, will be more hospita-

---

394. Interview, Department of Justice, June 22, 1973.

395. See, for example, Robert B. McKersie, *Minority Employment Patterns in an Urban Labor Market: The Chicago Experiment* (Washington: Equal Employment Opportunity Commission, 1972).

ble to affirmative action policies and increased minority employment. The longshore industry has always employed blacks, but, as has been shown, is a declining one in terms of employment. Many vestiges of segregation and racial discrimination persisted into the 1960's and in some cases, most notably in Texas, continued into the 1970's. Although blacks have not been excluded, their ability for both vertical and lateral movement within the industry has certainly been restricted. Moreover, it has taken direct government intervention, in the form of suits pursuant to Title VII of the Civil Rights Act of 1964, to force change upon recalcitrant union locals in order to achieve a more equitable division of available work in areas where black and white longshoremen have worked out of segregated locals and hiring halls.

Important, in this context, is that in those areas where the government has instituted legal action, blacks outnumber whites in the industry; yet whites were receiving more than one-half of all available work. In addition, although many more blacks were available for work, few, if any, served as clerks or checkers, the better, white collar jobs in the industry and only a few more were foremen or gang bosses. In this light it would be difficult to conclude that the longshore industry has been receptive to affirmative action policies.

In the years ahead, nevertheless, it appears likely that the black share of employment will expand. In ports such as New Orleans, whites are no longer seeking dock work in significant numbers. There still remain a substantially larger proportion of blacks than whites with little education and skill. High wages and until now steadier work on the longshore will continue to attract these blacks to the docks as whites look elsewhere.

Index